AF840275

Introduction to Occupational Psychiatry

Committee on Occupational Psychiatry
Group for the Advancement of Psychiatry

Barrie S. Greiff, M.D., Newton, MA, *Chairperson*
Peter L. Brill, M.D., Radnor, PA
Duane Q. Hagen, M.D., St. Louis, MO
R. Edward Huffman, M.D., Asheville, NC
Robert Larsen, M.D., San Francisco, CA
David E. Morrison, M.D., Palatine, IL
David B. Robbins, M.D., Chappaqua, NY
Jay B. Rohrlich, M.D., New York, NY
Clarence J. Rowe, M.D., St. Paul, MN
Jeffrey L. Speller, M.D., Cambridge, MA
Mark Unterberg, M.D., Dallas, TX, *Consultant*
Lenny Groopman, M.D., New York, NY, *Ginsburg Fellow*
Michael Paridis, M.D., Montreal, PQ, *Ginsburg Fellow*
Gabriel K. Wong, M.D., Honolulu, HI, *Ginsburg Fellow*

Introduction to Occupational Psychiatry

Formulated by the
Committee on Psychiatry in Industry

Group for the Advancement of Psychiatry

Report No. 138

Published by

American Psychiatric Press, Inc

Washington, DC
London, England

Copyright © 1994 Group for the Advancement of Psychiatry
ALL RIGHTS RESERVED

97 96 95 94 4 3 2 1

Published by American Psychiatric Press, Inc.
1400 K Street, N.W., Washington, DC 20005

Library of Congress Cataloging-in-Publication Data

Introduction to occupational psychiatry / formulated by the Committee on Psychiatry in Industry, Group for the Advancement of Psychiatry.
p. cm. — (Report ; no. 138).
Includes bibliographical references and index.
ISBN 0-87318-206-5
1. Industrial psychiatry. I. Group for the Advancement of Psychiatry. Committee on Psychiatry in Industry. II. Series: Report (Group for the Advancement of Psychiatry : 1994) ; no. 138.
[DNLM: 1. Occupational Medicine—United States. 2. Mental Health Services—United States. 3. Psychiatry. 4. United States. W1 RE209BR no. 138 1994 / WA 495 I618 1994]
RC321.G7 no. 138
[RC967.5]
616.89 s—dc20
[616.89]
DNLM/DLC
for Library of Congress 93-11640
CIP

British Library Cataloguing in Publication Data
A CIP record is available from the British Library.

Contents

Introduction vii

1 Models of Consultation for Occupational Psychiatrists . . 1

2 Rewards and Challenges 15

3 Pathways Into Occupational Psychiatry 23

4 Guidelines for the Occupational Psychiatrist 35

Afterword 39

Appendixes
- A—Psychiatric Work History 45
- B—Organizational History 49

Bibliography 57

GAP Committees and Membership 63

GAP Publications 77

Index 87

Introduction

In all areas of human endeavor, the naming of an activity usually comes after the fact. What we now call "occupational psychiatry" began in the 1920s, when a few individual psychiatrists were asked by industrial organizations to consult about productivity, morale, and problem employees. Over the years, groups of these psychiatrists came together to assist each other in this new, uncharted clinical endeavor, and because they felt a kinship with those company doctors who coined the name "occupational medicine," they called themselves "occupational psychiatrists."

It is for this historical reason that occupational psychiatry is generally associated with caring for employees in private-sector companies. Of course, psychiatrists who work with employees of government agencies, hospitals, prisons, unions, colleges, and the armed forces can rightly be called occupational psychiatrists as well, but these specialists have generally organized separately and given themselves different names: "prison psychiatrists," "military psychiatrists," "college psychiatrists," and so on.

Questions are frequently asked about the differences between "occupational" and "organizational" psychiatry. These are difficult to answer because the differences are primarily semantic, and the terms are often used interchangeably. "Organizational" is a broader, more inclusive term. However, if we understand the rather arbitrary and after-the-fact development of names for different activities, we can avoid getting too caught up in fine distinctions.

Our intention in this introduction is to stimulate interest in the field of occupational psychiatry among psychiatric residents and other psychiatrists. We hope to focus on the opportunities available to our colleagues in this area and to provide answers for career planning questions such as "How does a psychiatrist gain entree into an organization?" We want to acquaint fellow professionals with the rich literature in the field of occupational psychiatry, and we hope ultimately that the interest generated may help to create a need for fellowships and subspecialty training.

For the purposes of this book, we will define the occupational psychiatrist as *a psychiatrist who is interested in human behavior in the workplace, who directly or indirectly enters the organizational setting, and who functions at the dynamic interface between the employee and the organization.* He or she is concerned with the psychological impact of the workplace on the emotional health of the individual (or group of individuals), and with the psychological impact of individuals (or groups) on the quality of the functioning of the workplace. Even though, as we noted previously, any employee and any kind of work organization may come under the purview of the occupational psychiatrist, most of our examples here will come from profit-oriented industrial workplaces because of the historical roots of the field.

A Brief History of Occupational Psychiatry

Dr. Mandel Sherman of the Northwestern University Department of Psychiatry presented the first review of "industrial psychiatry" in the April 1927 *American Journal of Psychiatry*. His emphasis was primarily on individual intrapsychic conflict as it showed itself in the workplace. Companies at that time, however, largely eschewed the psychological and turned rather to technological and "human engineering" techniques (e.g., Taylor's so-called "time in motion" work) to resolve production problems. The major exception was the classic work of Elton Mayo and his colleagues at the Harvard Business School, who took a more humanistic approach to the industrial worker. Their research was conducted at the Hawthorne plant of Western Electric from 1929 to 1933.

The impact of World War II, with its tremendous production demands and the shortage of labor, required the use of individuals not usually considered employable in factory work (i.e., women, old people, and people with disabilities). This change accentuated interest in the psychiatric approach to industry, with the consequent decline in popularity of the human engineering approaches.

During the 1940s and 1950s, human relations in industry were associated with three primary schools of thought:

- The Elton Mayo School centered at the Harvard Business School, which emphasized the social system, the clinical approach, and the case method of teaching;
- The School of Applied Anthropology led by Elliot Chapple, William F. White, and Conrad Arensberg, which emphasized sound field work and social observation; and
- The Kurt Lewin School of Group Dynamics with its center at the University of Michigan and its affiliates at the Tavistock Institute of Human Relations in London and the National Training Laboratories in Washington, DC.

The first postresidency training for psychiatrists was established in 1948 at Cornell University's School of Industrial and Labor Relations. Specialized training in occupational psychiatry was offered at the Menninger Foundation and the University of Cincinnati.

The 1940s also were a time of keen interest on the part of psychoanalysts in the psychoanalysis of work. Ives Hendrick (1943) postulated a primary "mastery instinct." Menninger (1942) saw work as a sublimation of the aggressive drive. Other papers by Lantos (1943) and Oberndorf (1951) are critical contributions to our understanding of the deeper intrapsychic meanings of the drive to work.

The late 1950s and early 1960s was an extremely productive period in occupational psychiatry. A number of behavioral scientists at different centers began to achieve national recognition. The involvement of the American Psychiatric Association (APA) with psychiatry in the workplace drew international attention during 1959, when the Association's Committee on Occupational Psychiatry published a pamphlet entitled *Troubled People on the Job.*

In 1965, the National Institute of Mental Health created the National Clearinghouse for Mental Health Information and named occupational psychiatry as one of the 20 key topics to be researched and abstracted. The nature of the workplace in the late 1960s and early 1970s was influenced by the impact of a strong counterculture, the adoption of Title 7 of the Equal Employment Act of 1972, the emerging role of women in managerial roles, and the transition from a manufacturing to an informational society.

In the 1980s and early 1990s, psychiatrists continued to play a critical role in developing new models of mental health intervention. In 1985, Greiff established the Center for the Study of Work at the Institute of Living with four primary components: consultation, seminars, training, and research. In 1991, under the direction of Len Sperry, M.D., Ph.D., at the Medical College of Wisconsin, a fellowship was established in occupational and organizational psychiatry.

Work and the Occupational Psychiatrist

At least one-third of our lives is spent at work. It is the cause and cure of many of our ills. We feel loved through the admiration our work earns. We are empty and dejected when work fails. Goals we work toward define us; without them we lack purpose and direction. We discharge aggression when we attack our tasks, and our successes protect us from the debilitating stress of frustrated ambition. We feel masterful and strong in achievement, weak and impotent in failure. We earn our place in civilization through our work. We reduce guilt through hard labor and defy time with accomplishment. Work organizations structure our lives and, for many of us, the people we love, hate, fear, and need come as importantly from our offices, factories, and shops as from our families and communities.

Physicians care for individuals who are ill. To diagnose illness, we look for pathogens from the biological, social, and psychological spheres. Our work environments provide many of these. Powerful organizational forces act on people's psyches. Axis IV, in a DSM-III-R (American Psychiatric Association 1987) diagnosis, underscores psychosocial stressors in the creation and maintenance of psychiatric disorders. The world of work remains insufficiently appreciated as an arena through which emotional and mental disturbances may be generated, prevented, and treated.

In our opinion, psychiatrists have traditionally focused too narrowly on the personal, individual realm as their point of diagnostic and therapeutic entry. The purpose of this report is to emphasize the value of psychiatrists looking harder at the world of work, not only to appreciate more fully the "whole" patients they are dealing with, but also to be more effective in helping them.

Occupational psychiatrists have a primary concern with the mental health of employees. They study the effects of psychiatric disorders on the workplace, and the influence of the workplace on the mental status of employees, including aspects of the work environment that stimulate mentally *healthy* behavior. Occupational psychiatrists concern themselves with morale, job satisfaction, and specific occupational roles that may also be related to mental health in the work setting. They try to understand work in relation to the family, the community, and society.

A day in the life of an occupational psychiatrist may include evaluating a disabled worker with a major depression; doing a preemployment interview with a mental status evaluation; dealing with an obstreperous, disruptive employee; and intervening in a case of substance abuse on the job. He or she may meet for a few sessions with a gay executive who is upset about not getting the job he sought and who suspects bias. An occupational psychiatrist may be called on to resolve a dispute between two factory workers, for example, and is often asked to analyze the dynamics in a case of alleged sexual harassment or age discrimination. He or she may meet for a few sessions with an employee contemplating retirement, or one who has posttraumatic stress following a robbery in her store, or with a CEO who wants to expand his company.

In 1988, to determine the number of psychiatrists currently involved in industry or other work environments, the APA Task Force on Occupational Psychiatry placed a notice in *Psychiatric News* asking that psychiatrists practicing occupational psychiatry identify themselves to the task force. Approximately 100 responded. They were sent brief questionnaires inquiring about the nature, scope, and duration of their involvement; 77 were returned. Twenty-one percent of the respondents spent 80%–100% of their time in occupational psychiatry, whereas 67% spent less than half of their practice time in the field. Almost all respondents (94%) did some consulting and on the average worked with 5 organizations (the range was 1 to 20). Approximately 66% of the respondents were involved in some way with an employee assistance program (EAP). Most practiced in more than one setting; by far the most frequent was the office, and the least frequent were classrooms and research laboratories. The respondents' average length of involvement in the field of occupational psychiatry was 10.5 years, with a range of 3 months to 30 years; 29% of the respondents had been in the field for fewer than 5 years.

The APA Task Force on Occupational Psychiatry concluded:

> There is a risk to psychiatry [of losing touch with the world of patients] in not attending to the world of work. There is [economic] risk to industry if psychiatrists are not involved. If one element can characterize the work setting of the 1980s and 1990s, that element is change. Change, even change for the better, brings fear, stress, and misunderstanding. Because psychiatrists understand the psychic processes and the dynamics of growth, interpersonal interactions, and the influences of external forces on the individual, they have the unique opportunity to work with management and labor alike to ensure that the inevitable change in the work environment is positive. (APA Council on National Affairs 1984, p. 1,139)

Traditionally, psychiatrists have been perceived as physicians administering to mentally ill people in the office or hospital setting. But psychiatry broke with the traditional model of reactive, intensive, long-term treatment over 30 years ago. With the start of the community mental health movement and its related emphasis on prevention, psychiatry became concerned with the functioning of individuals in their environments. Although this movement had many positive consequences, it failed to live up to expectations. Poverty, deinstitutionalization, and conflict between different mental health professions, along with many other social, political, and economic causes, interfered with the mission to provide primary, secondary, and tertiary interventions to large populations.

Within the past decade, however, there has been a significant shift in emphasis to the workplace as the locus for psychiatric intervention. This is due in part to the industrialization of American psychiatry (Bittker 1985), which involves the increased recognition of work as a critical variable in the mental health of the individual. The role of the psychiatrist has broadened to include an interest in organizational dynamics.

However, the humanitarian mission of occupational psychiatry does not automatically convince policy makers of its necessity, particularly those who pay the bills: government, business, and other third-party payors. They demand evidence of the benefits of health programs, rather than passively accepting the suggestions of well-meaning proponents. The nature of the research from the field has been clinical and descriptive. More systematic, quantitative studies, particularly those focused on the outcome of occupational psychiatric interventions, remain to be done.

The impact of mental illness on absenteeism, morale, productivity, and physical health has been well documented. *The Special Report to Congress of the National Institute of Drug and Alcohol Abuse* estimated, in 1983, that the yearly cost to American business of alcoholism, chemical dependency, and mental illness was $102 billion. As enlightened organizations have begun to institute programs in the workplace to deal with these problems, these losses have been diminished. It is variously estimated that every $1 spent on mental health programs in industry leads to saving $3–5 in reduced medical benefit payouts, reduced absenteeism, diminished retraining, and increased productivity (Gaeta et al. 1982; Hearle 1989). For example, the McDonnell-Douglas Corporation in St. Louis, carefully assessed individual cases and emphasized quality care from the outset of their programs; as a result, they expect to save more than $5 million in the next 3 years. During the past 4 years, employees who used the EAP for chemical dependency treatment missed 47% fewer workdays, had 81% lower attrition, and filed an average $10,300 per employee less in health care claims than those who did not use the EAP. Savings were somewhat smaller in all categories for psychiatric care. ("Spending to cut mental health costs" 1989).

Related fields of organizational development have much to contribute to occupational psychiatry. The work of McGregor (1967), Levinson (1962), Simon (1960), Argyris (1960), Trist (1963), and Herzberg (1966) provides valuable insight into the lives of people at work. Many leaders of corporations are wise, highly motivated, creative, and caring individuals who face difficult choices and stresses and who accept direct responsibility for influencing the lives of their workers. The failure of psychiatrists to establish a meaningful alliance with these leaders of industry will result in a significant loss to both groups.

Although nonpsychiatric health care workers have important skills and make important contributions to employee-patient well-being, the lack of medical and psychiatric input into the evaluation, referral, and treatment process has profound implications for the absence of biological input into the biopsychosocial status of the employee (Report of the Committee on Occupational Psychiatry 1989; Trist 1963). Currently, a rapidly growing component of the American Psychological Association is organizational psychology. In addition, there is a large and strong movement of EAPs. These programs are contractual relationships with organizations to provide evaluation referral, and sometimes treatment, for all employees of an organization. The number of these programs has grown from 50 to several thousand over the past 10 years. Almost none of these organizations has a physician, and virtually none has psychiatric involvement. Of the two largest national programs, each providing services to 1 million employees, one is entirely run by social workers and the other by psychologists.

Summing Up

Psychiatry, if it is to respond to the whole person, must become increasingly aware of the lives of individuals in work settings. A number of clinicians and researchers (Center for Occupational Psychiatry in San Francisco; Greiff 1978; Greiff and Munter 1980; Rohrlich 1980) have documented the reciprocal relationship between personal and work dynamics. Kanter (1977) has challenged "the myth of separate worlds"—that is, the notion that work organizations operate independently of individual and family life. The unreality of this myth is painfully obvious in the catastrophic personal and family effects of unemployment, the decline of obsolescent industries (so-called "sunset" industries), and of plant closings. It is also obvious in the impact on the family of the intense overwork of the successful "workaholic" (Rohrlich 1980).

In 1920, E. E. Southard stated: "Industrial Medicine exists, Industrial Psychiatry ought to exist. It is important for the modern psychiatrist not to hide his light under a bushel; he must step forth to more community duties" (p. 550). In 1984, Nancy Roeske reaffirmed this issue: "Medicine and business are two separate cultures within our society. Ideologically they are polarized and attract people with different personality structures and value systems. Yet the necessity for work alliances has become inevitable."

1

Models of Consultation for Occupational Psychiatrists

Labor in loneliness is irksome.

Mark Twain
The Innocents Abroad

The essence of occupational psychiatry is the simultaneous focus on the individual and the organization. The psychiatrist's advisory and therapeutic effort straddles the dynamic interface between both, attempting to find an optimal balance. This role has many unique features that may separate it from more traditional psychiatric ones. According to Levinson (1972), the occupational psychiatrist generally

- Shifts orientation from pathology to prevention and motivation;
- Relies less on interpretation and confrontation than on counseling and advice;
- Introduces a psychological orientation into business decision making;
- Is often more active than receptive; and
- Becomes integrated into someone else's system, including understanding the business culture and language.

Confidentiality and trust are sensitive issues for the occupational psychiatrist. He or she must gain the respect and cooperation of all parties even though their respective needs may be (or at least appear to be) in conflict.

This also means attending to the irrationalities of the parties concerned. Work, as Freud (1930/1962) contended, attaches people to external reality; but infantile fantasies and feelings about survival also arise directly from our work experience, and corporate irrationalities are no less a factor to contend with than is individual irrationality. Furthermore, in the role of juggler, the occupational psychiatrist must also integrate the languages of business and medical psychology. Concepts such as absenteeism, productivity, and morale are woven into the more familiar ideas of depression, anxiety, transference, and conflict.

The occupational psychiatrist may be a part-time or full-time employee or a self-employed consultant. He or she may function as an advisor to the chief executive or work within the human resources and/or medical departments. After entry (various means of entry are outlined in Chapter 3), the occupational psychiatrist becomes part of the corporate landscape in a variety of ways. Various communication media are used to announce his or her availability to employees. These include brochures, seminars, workshops, and management, personnel, or medical meetings.

After their "psychological" acceptance by the organization, psychiatrists are often consulted spontaneously about personal problems, personnel issues, and group conflicts. By their very presence in the company, occupational psychiatrists allow emotions to be a legitimate area of individual and organizational concern. When problems arise, the emotional ramifications may be recognized, as psychiatrists create the structure in which to deal with them.

The occupational psychiatrist needs a flexible theoretical orientation. General systems theory, with a focus on the interrelationships of subsystems and levels of organizations, allows the occupational psychiatrist to integrate data ranging from individual psychodynamics to small and large social systems. As we shall observe in the following case histories, a prime ingredient in the consultant's repertoire of skills is the ability to define the most appropriate level of intervention in a complex structure. This position is not a call for haphazard eclecticism. We are describing a conceptual orientation encompassing intrapsychic, interpersonal, small group, and organizational dynamics. For illustration, we have selected five points on the occupational psychiatry consultation continuum as models of intervention:

1. Dyadic consultation—the traditional office model.
2. Liaison consultation—individual focus but involving others in the organization.
3. Expanded consultation—initial individual focus with expansion into organization intervention.
4. Team consultation—small group/interpersonal focus.
5. Strategic consultation—corporate structure and policy.

Dyadic Consultation

The first model of psychiatric consultation has many similarities to ordinary psychotherapy, but the emphasis in the chief complaint and in the content of the therapy is the patient's *work*. The setting may be a private office away from or on the worksite, and the patient is usually self-referred. Occupational issues are highlighted and career progression examined in a developmental perspective. A careful assessment, including the patient's work history (Kates et al. 1990) and organizational history (Levinson 1972), includes details of job function and work environment, income, and interpersonal relationships with managers, co-workers, subordinates, and competitors. In cases in which the chief complaint is anxiety or depression, dynamic psychotherapy often reveals that the workplace is a major catalyst of internal conflict. Therapy may be brief and focused on specific occupational conflicts, or the intervention may evolve into long-term psychotherapy, depending on what is clinically and/or practically appropriate. The following case exemplifies this model.

Case 1

Mr. A., a 52-year-old marketing specialist, was referred for psychiatric consultation by his private internist because of Mr. A.'s lethargy and progressive loss of interest in his family and job during the previous 6 months. Mr. A.'s private internist served part-time as an occupational physician and was alert to work-related issues. In addition, he had collaborated with the occupational psychiatrist on several previous occasions.

During the year preceding psychiatric consultation, Mr. A. had a series of losses and disappointments. After an unsuccessful trial of living in his son's home, Mr. A.'s father died in a nursing home at age 90. Guilt over placing his father in the home complicated Mr. A.'s grief, although his father had agreed that his failing strength and declining ability to care for himself clearly warranted an institutional placement. Within a few months, Mr. A.'s dog died after a companionship of 14 years. These losses complicated a troubled marriage, damaged by his wife's alcohol abuse.

The ultimate stress that led to Mr. A.'s symptoms and psychiatric referral, however, was the dissolution of the company department in which he had worked for 13 years and his consequent transfer to a lower-level marketing support role. Soon after this occurred, Mr. A. noted the gradual onset of lassitude and feeling "punched out," with progressive loss of interest in his work, home life, and previously pleasurable activities.

Treatment consisted of individual, dynamic psychotherapy with emphasis on the interplay of family and work losses. During 12 months of psychotherapy, Mr. A. explored the complex interrelationships of his marriage and his work. He came to realize that he had escaped from an unsatisfactory marriage by progressively devoting his interest and energy to work activities. His self-esteem became progressively dependent on work success. Mr. A. played a major part in the development of his department and the training of colleagues and subordinates. When he was forced to return to a marketing support role, he felt betrayed and abandoned. It became apparent that he could not simultaneously cope with the loss of his father and the loss of his work family.

As psychotherapy progressed, Mr. A.'s energy and commitment to new professional activities improved. He was able to assist his wife in her recovery from alcohol abuse and rebuild his marital commitments. At the same time he became more actively involved in new work activities for which he received increasing recognition.

This form of occupational psychiatry practice differs from traditional psychotherapy only in the fact that the clinical material comes primarily from the work arena, even though there is no direct collaboration with the patient's work organization. The patient's own clinical improvement suffices to correct the situation.

Liaison Consultation

Individual evaluation with ancillary consultation to corporate medical and personnel departments, as well as to management, is the second type of occupational psychiatric intervention. The patients may be self-referred or recommended by medical staff, employee assistance counselors, managers, union representatives, or others. In this liaison model, although the psychiatrist focuses on the fit of the employee and his or her work environment, primary attention is paid to the worker's strengths and limitations. In contrast to expanded consultation, no effort is made to change the organization. The liaison model is illustrated by the following two case vignettes.

Case 2

The occupational psychiatrist serving as a consultant to a bank was summoned to an urgent meeting in the office of the Vice President of Personnel. A secretary, Ms. B., had filed a complaint about her boss, a Senior Vice President of the bank. Several nights before, while working late, the Senior Vice President, Mr. C., called Ms. B. into his office, asked her to come behind his desk, and exposed himself to her. She became frightened, ran out of the office, and took 2 days off from work. Before returning to her job, Ms. B. presented herself to the Personnel Department, demanding that she be given a new job within the organization and that Mr. C. be fired. She said that she could not return to her job until this was done.

The psychiatrist met with Ms. B., who was a 35-year-old single African American woman with a college degree. Ms. B. described a cordial, respectful, and proper 5-year working relationship with her boss. There had never been any suggestion of overt sexual interest on either person's part. Ms. B. was bewildered and angry, and she felt degraded by what Mr. C. had done. She also intimated that racism was also a factor in his behavior.

The psychiatrist subsequently interviewed Ms. B.'s boss. Mr. C. was ashamed, remorseful, and depressed. He said he had never done anything like this before, and he claimed that he did not understand the sudden impulse that came over him that evening. In the course of the interview, Mr. C. confessed that two things had been tormenting him for the past several months: he had discovered that his wife was having an affair, and he acknowledged that he was deeply in debt. Mr. C. did not know how to confront his wife either about her affair or the fact that a bank was preparing to foreclose on their home mortgage. After these interviews, the occupational psychiatrist carefully weighed the data, evaluated the relationships among Ms. B., Mr. C., and the bank, and then concluded with the following recommendations to management:

1. The psychiatrist would consult with senior management and the Personnel Department. The Personnel Department should consider the psychological impact on the various parties involved of firing Mr. C. for sexual harassment, which might be the organization's responsibility.
2. Mr. C. and Ms. B. should each be referred for individual psychotherapy.
3. Mr. C. should be given guidance and assistance with his personal finances.
4. The possibility (albeit remote) of a restoration of the formerly good working relationship between these two people should be explored. This would include an appreciation of the emotional wounds of both people. Involved employees would be assisted in preventing destructive information from spreading through the department and the organization.
5. Groups should be organized, perhaps led by the psychiatrist, to discuss issues of sexual harassment and racism at the bank.

By limiting disclosure to information needed for business purposes, the psychiatrist explained the situation to the executive and personnel officers in charge without compromising Mr. C.'s privacy. Mr. C. began psychotherapeutic treatment with an outside psychiatrist. The bank helped him restructure his debts and refinance his mortgage. He and Ms. B., after several meetings with the psychiatrist, reestablished a respectful but permanently altered relationship. Because the matter had come to the attention of some of the people in the department, senior management and the Personnel Department decided to transfer Mr. C. to a new position in a different area so that the issue would not serve as a potentially disruptive distraction to the department. Ms. B. remained in her position.

In this example, the occupational psychiatrist actively operated in the dynamic interface between the individual and the work organization. He addressed the personal needs of Ms. B. and Mr. C. simultaneously with the bank's requirements for the smooth operation of business. The focus was entirely on individual and organizational adjustment—not, as we shall see in cases using expanded consultation, on organizational change.

Case 3

A programming manager for an information retrieval group called the Medical Department. He was concerned about one of his employees, a systems analyst, Ms. D., whom he had recently hired. She had years of experience, superior technical skills, and a solid reputation, yet she was failing. The manager told the occupational psychiatrist, who was employed part-time by the company, that Ms. D. was often late, complained of fatigue, yet apparently wanted to contribute her valuable skills to the group. The psychiatrist asked the manager for a detailed description of Ms. D.'s job responsibilities, both technical and interpersonal. With the psychiatrist's guidance, they focused their dialogue on the employee-job fit. Then Ms. D. was asked to visit the Medical Department for psychiatric consultation.

When they met the next morning, the psychiatrist was struck by Ms. D.'s aura of "doom and gloom." She spoke of her increasing sense of desperation as she then came to believe that she could never meet the needs of her manager and his department. She had difficulty sleeping, noted a definite loss of energy, and felt that her work was compromised by ongoing difficulties with concentration and short-term memory.

A quiet, introspective, single woman in her 30s, Ms. D. was someone who placed enormous value on her leisure time. She was a lover of culture and frequently attended concerts and art shows. Her social life centered on friends in her condominium community. Ms. D. lived alone and had no relatives nearby. As clarified in the detailed interview, in her new job she was expected to adapt to long hours, frequent emergency design requirements, and tight time constraints. This assignment frequently prevented her from participating in community activities. Ms. D. remembered her previous position with a sense of pain and loss. It had been a well-structured, comfortably paced, and intellectually rewarding job. Most importantly, it did not interfere with her personal life. During the interview, Ms. D. started to cry. She thought that accepting this assignment was one of the worst mistakes of her career. Although Ms. D.'s social adaptation capacity was constricted, the occupational psychiatrist understood corporate culture sufficiently to conclude that the principal problem was a mismatch of this person and her current job.

Ms. D. concurred with this formulation and asked for help in finding a new position in the company. In the next few months, the occupational psychiatrist and Ms. D. met several times to review her job search. With his assistance, she became better able to discuss her personal needs and job goals with her new manager, and the psychiatrist's involvement in this story gradually ended when Ms. D. received her transfer.

Expanded Consultation

On some occasions individual consultation extends into corporate program development, education, or policy determination. The clinician is asked to see an individual in the organization because of symptomatic behavior. As the occupational psychiatrist investigates both the individual and the organization, he or she learns that the peculiar problems presented by the patient may be a function of more generalized conflicts within the company. Accordingly, the occupational psychiatrist broadens the intervention to include personnel specialists, managers, and human resource educators. A variety of systematic organizational changes may result. This progression is illustrated by the following two clinical examples.

Case 4

A normally energetic Vice President of a large corporation, Mr. E., had become angry, anxious, and troubled by stomach pain. He contacted the Medical Department doctor and, after a brief history and physical examination, he was referred to the occupational psychiatrist. Mr. E. had been concerned about poor morale among his company's security guards. In his search for a remedy, he was intrigued by a story he had read about a security force that wore blazers instead of traditional blue uniforms.

Mr. E. decided that substituting smart-looking business jackets for uniforms would be good for his staff's morale and might also reduce the transfer of community antipolice feelings to his security force. Without consulting the security guards, Mr. E. told the personnel manager to choose and order the blazers.

Two weeks after the blazers arrived, only one man had worn his blazer for more than 3 consecutive days; most of the jackets had to be altered and occasionally even altered again. Numerous buttons "just came off." One blazer was severely damaged in an altercation. Another guard said he would not wear such a "sissy-looking" outfit. Still another said he would quit. One employee, who was recovering from alcoholism with 6 years of sobriety, was located in a distant rehabilitation facility after 10 days of unexplained absence. Finally, a petition signed by all of the guards requesting a return of the old uniform was sent to Mr. E.

In his first consultation with Mr. E., the occupational psychiatrist took a careful history of the organization's development. He then secured a personal history from Mr. E., with particular focus on his career development. The psychiatrist wanted to evaluate the extent to which the present problem was simply a miscalculation of Mr. E.'s, or whether it was part of a more enduring managerial or personality pattern. Did he have an irrational need for control? Did he make precipitous decisions or have a history of conflict with prior groups? No such patterns were uncovered. The interview also carefully considered the possibility that the current problem was part of a lifelong personality pattern. The question of Mr. E.'s current circumstances at home possibly contributing to the situation at work was investigated. Again, this revealed nothing remarkable.

Having obtained adequate information from Mr. E., the psychiatrist began weekly group meetings with the security guards, initially to discuss their morale problems. In this forum, specific issues regarding salary, bonuses, recognition, racial prejudice, and other topics were openly explored. The guards developed sufficient confidence to resolve some of these conflicts directly with Mr. E. The psychiatrist also made direct recommendations to Mr. E. These included more open communication with his employees and greater consideration of their wishes, including a return to their traditional uniforms. The psychiatrist served as facilitator in meetings that addressed both communication and management problems between the guards and the rest of the company's management.

As the consultation process proceeded, Mr. E.'s distress subsided and, gradually, his complaints and symptoms cleared. The company also developed a more open and comfortable relationship between senior management and staff. The lessons learned from the blazer episode had been applied to reworking the company's corporate culture and structure.

Case 5

The occupational psychiatrist was asked by the Plant Director to evaluate a middle manager, Mr. F., because of a recent change in the manager's behavior. In an initial interview with the director, the psychiatrist was told that Mr. F. had become sullen, tense, and irritable. His colleagues suspected that he was abusing alcohol. Because of significant performance failures, Mr. F. was about to be separated from the company. In his first meeting with Mr. F., the psychiatrist clarified the purposes of the evaluation, including the modifications of confidentiality occasioned by his performance difficulties.

The interviews revealed that Mr. F. was an angry, depressed man who was uncomplimentary and critical of his immediate superior and the Plant Director. Mr. F. had significant family problems overlapping his drinking (which he admitted to) and declining work performance. Following the evaluation, the occupational psychiatrist referred Mr. F. to a colleague for formal psychiatric treatment.

As treatment progressed, the occupational psychiatrist served as a liaison among the treating psychiatrist, Mr. F., and the company. Because of positive results and subsequent deepening trust, the Plant Director consulted with the occupational psychiatrist about his own personal concerns, particularly his relations with his executive team.

The occupational psychiatrist was able to study the dynamics of the organization. Consulting relationships were developed with several other senior managers in which their personal needs as well as the organization's problems were explored. This progressive expansion of consultation occurred over several months. It turned out that some of the employees' original perceptions regarding the plant were accurate. The working environment was not supportive, individuals had unclear roles, and communication between functional departments ranged from difficult to nonexistent. The psychiatrist began by identifying the relationship problems in the top team and then worked on clarifying the type of environment they wished to have.

By working through the relationships on an interpersonal and organizational basis, the atmosphere below the top team began to improve. Interdepartmental barriers began to diminish, and a generally more supportive environment evolved. With each intervention, the occupational psychiatrist learned more about the company's dynamics. He assisted several executives in coping with difficult economic and political changes. Not only had the occupational psychiatrist, in conjunction with the psychotherapist, resolved Mr. F.'s problem, but the whole operation had left the organization healthier for all concerned.

Team Consultation

The next phase in the Occupational Consultation continuum consists of diagnostic and therapeutic interventions at the interpersonal, small group, operational level. In this model, the corporate organization is the focus of study and investigation. The psychiatrist interviews many people, individually and in small groups, and examines business data, including the annual report, the table of organization, and yearly department summaries. If personal problems surface, individuals may be referred to therapy. The psychiatrist often prepares a report with formal recommendations and proposals. Ideally, he or she educates members of the organization to continue the therapeutic process themselves. An example of this type of consultation follows.

Case 6

The occupational psychiatrist met the director of a technical division in a large corporation during a 5-day retreat and seminar organized for executives. Some time later, the director asked for ideas to assist his people in stress management. They agreed to a series of seminars and small group discussions for senior executives. As the dialogue proceeded, the psychiatrist learned that the technology of this division was desperately needed by other divisions, but was very threatening to them.

The technical division management was said to be more interested in science and engineering than in people; they handled employee responsibilities reluctantly. Because the senior executives of the parent corporation were ambivalent about their dependency on the technical division, they offered little help and guidance. These initial seminars not only helped the employees become better able to cope with stress, they also familiarized the occupational psychiatrist with the culture and problems of the division and of the company itself.

The psychiatrist advised the top executives on how to reduce stress by internal change in divisional management practices and policy, and the technical division was integrated more comfortably into the company structure. Six months after the last seminar, the occupational psychiatrist saw one of the division Vice Presidents about personal and corporate issues. Other senior division managers followed, and they revealed marital, developmental, and business problems. The occupational psychiatrist used brief counseling to help these individuals cope better on a personal as well as professional basis, thereby raising the adaptive competency of many key members of the company. Some people were referred for long-term therapy. This is often an essential step in preparation for significant organizational improvement.

Next, the psychiatrist initiated monthly visits to the facility. He reviewed the information gleaned from his consultation with a number of executives and had new and useful insights that were relevant to organizational problems. He continued counseling individual groups on coping with change, and he designed and operated management development sessions. He also participated in retreats and also provided emergency consultation and services.

Many difficult interpersonal and structural issues were resolved. Tactical Organizational Units were strengthened; destructive behavior not ameliorated by psychotherapeutic intervention was administratively resolved. For example,

1. Two recalcitrant Vice Presidents with poor people and planning skills were confronted, offered support, and (after a reasonable time) were released when they did not change their behavior. They were replaced with more sensitive and more realistic managers. The occupational psychiatrist was involved in offering guidance to the two difficult employees, but management made the termination decisions after a lack of positive change.
2. One manager made remarkable interpersonal and managerial changes. Projective tests revealed improved reality testing and psychosexual development. He became an obvious successor to the Executive Vice President.
3. Other interventions coped with suicide and other self-destructive behaviors, sexual acting-out behavior, major organizational growth, two recessions, and pressure from the parent corporation.

After the formal sessions ended, the occupational psychiatrist and the Executive Vice President continued to communicate on a monthly basis. The management team was able to further their development and effectiveness by utilizing techniques learned during the active phases of psychiatric intervention.

Strategic Consultation

The final model consists of psychiatric consultation with senior management to examine corporate structure, policy, and philosophy. Close collaboration among the psychiatrist, directors, and chief executive and operating officers allows the consultant to learn how the organization adapts to change, resolves conflicts, and implements policy. At this level the consultant can influence decisions that affect the entire work force. Issues can include the mental health implications of hiring and firing, acquisitions and takeovers, conflict resolution, cutbacks, relocations, health benefits, and contract negotiations. Consultation at the level of strategic management broadens the opportunity for primary prevention, because at this level the consultant can influence decisions that affect the entire work force. Because modern business depends on the motivation, flexibility, and productivity of its employees, it is essential that the management of the social processes of the organization flows smoothly with the technical requirements of the organization.

To function expertly in this consulting role, the psychiatrist must be aware of organizational structure and politics, including the maintenance of appropriate boundaries. The consultant should continuously formulate his or her psychological contract with the organization and clarify the consulting role and appropriate behavior. Intrusion into management responsibilities vitiates the consulting process. Helping an organization clarify problems and find solutions parallels the psychotherapeutic work of individual treatment. The following two cases are examples of strategic consultation.

Case 7

A psychiatrist was asked to determine the causes and suggest actions to reduce a very high absenteeism and turnover rate at a large shipyard in the South. He spent 17 continuous days on site, averaging 12 hours a day studying the problem. He interviewed all the senior managers of the shipyard and collected data from hourly employees through a job attitude survey. The occupational psychiatrist was a participant observer in the application and hiring processes of hourly workers in the shipyard. He toured the entire facility and all of its subdivisions. As the occupational psychiatrist examined and studied the data, he discovered that the shipyard hourly work force over the previous 10 years had had a large influx of workers who were inexperienced, unskilled, uneducated, single African American males between the ages of 18 and 22 for whom shipyard jobs were their first steady employment. Forty-four percent of the absenteeism was attributed to the hourly workers who were under the age of 25, and 60% of the absenteeism was attributed to the hourly workers with less than 2 years of service.

The hourly workers voiced their dissatisfaction with the following issues:

1. Difficult and dangerous work;
2. Unsafe and unpleasant working conditions;
3. Below-average compensation and benefits package;
4. Lack of adequate job training; and
5. Poor relationships with supervisors who were older white Southern males.

The occupational psychiatrist concluded with the following, admittedly ideal, recommendations:

1. Safe and pleasant working conditions for the hourly work force;
2. Improvements in the salary and benefits for the hourly worker;
3. Introduction of a more effective recruitment and hiring process;

4. Development of an in-house training program emphasizing basic education, job, and interpersonal skills;
5. Introduction of supervisory education in African American history and culture, interpersonal skills, and conflict resolution; and
6. Development of performance evaluation criteria for managers tied to improvements in the quality of work life for all the employees and decreases in absenteeism and turnover.

In a year's time, after implementation of many of the occupational psychiatrist's recommendations, the absenteeism and turnover rate had been reduced by 40%.

Case 8

The consultant was contacted by Mr. G., the Divisional President of a large computer company. Mr. G. had attended a training session led by the consultant 7 years earlier, and he had found it beneficial. He had been promoted several times since the training session, and his division was responsible for two-thirds of the domestic business of the computer company. The situation Mr. G. was dealing with was very complex and difficult. The company had been formed by merging two large computer companies. The cost of the merger, coupled with increased competition in the computer industry internationally, had placed the company in a difficult economic position. Employees still identified with their original organization as a legacy of the merger. Furthermore, the new company determined they had too many employees compared to the competition, which necessitated multiple layoffs and constant restructuring. The top officers of the corporation vacillated, and many of them left.

It was within this context that Mr. G.'s role began to emerge. He had taken over a smaller division and had developed a strategy that turned that division around. Now he was given a much larger task. He had a clear strategy of what needed to be done. He spent the first several months in direct contact with most of his top and middle managers. Their demoralization was so deep that Mr. G. believed specialized help was required—thus his request for consultation. The occupational psychiatrist was assigned a full-time internal person trained in organizational development to assist in the task. Together they interviewed at all levels of the organization. Questionnaire data were collected, providing a quantitative picture of the organization climate and employee attitudes that were compared with national and industry norms.

Most employees thought that their psychological contract with the organization was violated. This partly conscious and partly unconscious contract, which consisted of perceptions, expectations, and identifications, apparently promised job security in return for employees' loyalty and investment in their jobs. Layoffs had ruptured this contract, leaving the employees insecure, angry, and reluctant to invest energy in the company. Also, many had "survivor's guilt" because they still had jobs and their friends were gone. Many were symptomatic with anxiety, depression, and psychosomatic complaints. Finally, the repeated reorganizations had left them confused as to what direction the company needed to follow. The consultant believed that the solution to these problems required the following:

1. Employees needed to develop a new philosophy about organizational life. This philosophy embraced change and risk as normal and expectable.
2. Employees needed to be taught to adapt faster to change.
3. Employees needed to be taught better coping skills for dealing with stress.
4. Managers needed to focus more on their own development and enhance their leadership skills. Although the managerial skills had been adequate for stable environments, leadership skills were essential during these times of turbulence.
5. Managers and employees needed to form rapidly supportive networks throughout the organization.
6. Conscious and unconscious guilt and anxiety resulting from layoffs required further working through.
7. The managerial team needed to accept Mr. G.'s decision and strategy for the future and needed to foster it in their employees.
8. Managers needed to understand and embrace strategies to lift employee morale.
9. The division needed to feel a sense of teamwork, collaborating to solve business and human problems.

To this end, the occupational psychiatrist and his internal counterpart developed a series of seminars for the top 150 managers in the company nationwide. Thirty managers at a time attended these seminars, followed by a second seminar 5 months later. Mr. G. required that all 150 of his top people attend, and he participated in the second round of every seminar.

The results from a business perspective were impressive. Not only did company morale improve greatly, but the division became highly successful. The managers made a commitment to the company, the division, Mr. G., and each other. They worked on their leadership skills and found creative solutions to help employees who worked for them.

The consultant's belief was that the psychiatric benefits included

1. Prevention or lessening of psychological illness;
2. Development of greatly increased psychological maturity and interpersonal skills; and
3. Development of greatly increased adaptational capacity.

2

Rewards and Challenges

> Work was for him, in The Nature of Things, the most estimable attribute of Life.
>
> Thomas Mann
> *The Magic Mountain*

Practicing in the world of work has significant rewards and challenges. This section focuses primarily on private-sector, profit-driven organizations, because that is where most of the new opportunities arise and where psychiatrists in general have had the least experience. Governmental and even not-for-profit organizations share many of the characteristics of for-profit firms, but many of their goals are different. However, in either case understanding the culture of the organization in which one practices is essential to success in this field. As the psychiatrist gains more complete knowledge of the traditions, values, and goals of a company, he or she will understand the economic, social, and political pressures impinging upon the individuals running it and working in it.

Business organizations pursue profit. Other goals—such as social responsibility, community involvement, employee satisfaction, and equal opportunity—are secondary. Individuals in management positions are responsible for the organization's profitable survival in a highly competitive environment. Introspection and human relationships have traditionally not been emphasized in profit-oriented companies. Most managers in industrial organizations today, however, can see the economic worth of these values when they are presented in understandable terms that do not conflict with the organization's mission. Helping these managers to understand the relevance of such values and then to pragmatically apply them in the workplace can be very rewarding.

The rewards of getting involved in an organizational culture are numerous, and the opportunities to help are great. There is also the chance to contribute to the well-being of people who may be very different from the psychiatrist's own private practice population. They include employees of various socioeconomic, ethnic, and racial groups in a wide variety of local, national, and even international companies who might not seek office psychotherapy on their own, even if they have insurance. The stimulation of working in settings away from the private office, clinic, or hospital can be highly gratifying.

The occupational psychiatrist has an opportunity to work at the interface of several different conceptual areas. Issues of mental health and mental illness in the workplace inevitably involve the interplay of the following:

- Employee intrapsychic conflicts;
- Interpersonal and small group dynamics;
- Organizational policies and procedures;
- Social structure, corporate culture, leadership issues; and
- Biological issues (e.g., toxicity, stressful elements in the workplace).

Traditional collaborations are often supplemented by working with human resource professionals, occupational physicians, professional trainers, and management. These provide significant advantages for occupational psychiatrists to broaden and enhance their skills. Invitations to lecture on unique workplace issues to groups such as medical students, psychiatric residents, and professional associations may arise (see Chapter 3 on these opportunities). In addition, some occupational psychiatrists teach courses at universities or work in schools of social work, psychology, education, and business administration. Depending on the availability of funds, there also may be opportunities to initiate research projects involving such issues as stress in the workplace, dual careers, working at home, disability, relocation, business travel, and the impact of mergers and acquisitions and downsizing on organizational life. At one time or another, the occupational psychiatrist may teach a course on executive stress in the retailing industry, investigate the special requirements for work and life on an oil drilling platform, consult with the senior management of an investment banking firm about a junior account executive who suddenly ran up a large debt (as the initial sign of cocaine addiction), or be involved in a sexual discrimination problem within the organization.

With a foundation in biological, psychological, and social sciences, the occupational psychiatrist is uniquely equipped to teach programs on job stress, drug and alcohol abuse, management of violence, and interpersonal relationships in families and at work. He or she may work with others in resolving issues of low morale and reduced productivity. The occupational psychiatrist has the perspective of recognizing the interplay of self, family, and work life on the productivity of the individual and the group. At the same time, he or she also may participate in a number of areas in which the psychiatrist is not an expert (e.g., information systems, compensation programs, severance, and deployment of the work force).

In summary, occupational psychiatry offers satisfaction from the level of individual clinical care to organizational policy making and management on the grand scale. Opportunities for professional fulfillment are enormous. With experience, simply mastering the multiple challenges faced in this work can become, in itself, one of the more gratifying aspects of the field of occupational consultation.

Nevertheless, there are significant obstacles for psychiatrists who want to work with organizations. Corporations may initially resist dealing with the psychiatrist even when such consultation is requested. Barriers that prevent a full consultation may unconsciously be established. These include missed appointments and limited information. Resistance may be due at times to the ambivalence of the organization requesting the consultation; it may also have to do with issues of trust.

Management may harbor feelings of guilt that they have played a role in the creation of psychiatric impairment among its employees, much like parents might feel about their disturbed child. They may resist becoming exposed and might be sensitive to psychiatrists who could reveal their "mistakes" and "flaws." A senior manager may take the stance, "If I'm a competent executive running a successful company, then I should be able to handle personnel problems myself." Such an individual sees any call for help as a sign of "managerial weakness."

Other managers may discharge an employee rather than try to understand him or her, or managers may try to "use" the psychiatrist as a way of implementing their decision. Although they are not typical "employees," of 610 psychiatric patients who were soldiers in a study of Vietnam duty (Huffman 1970), 26% were recommended for disciplinary action or separation from the service. The clear message from the "boss" was "not back in *my* shop." There is often a feeling in organizations that psychiatric consultation is too expensive and not efficient in dealing with a troubled employee. As one manager stated, "If they can't work here under our conditions, we'll find others who can."

A number of employees are often resistant to using on-site mental health services because of concerns about confidentiality. Although information on self-referred employees should always be kept absolutely private, they fear that information about them will leak and the organization will label them as emotionally unstable, leaving them in a vulnerable position and precluding their opportunities for advancement. Employees worry about the stigma that their fellow employees attach to utilization of mental health services. Many emotionally troubled employees fear that to seek professional help will raise questions in the minds of their peers about their judgment and ability.

Confidentiality concerns and the sometimes irrational, sometimes well-founded fears about lack of confidentiality and the consequences of disclosure pose significant obstacles to the establishment of a comfortable employee-occupational psychiatrist alliance.

> The physician's primary responsibility in [the occupational] setting is to maintain clarity regarding the purpose of the relationship. . . . The psychiatrist should not mislead the employee being evaluated by implying that the traditional doctor-patient relationship exists where it does not. This becomes very clear in Occupational Psychiatry when we are asked to render opinions on medical-legal issues for workers claiming psychiatric injury. Of primary importance in this role is the clinician's responsibility to inform the employee of the *lack* of confidentiality. (Larsen 1988, p. 721)

However, in our experience, management referrals of employees to the occupational psychiatrist are made out of sincere concern for the worker, with the wish that he or she be assisted to return to work more effectively. Only in infrequent cases is the psychiatrist asked to evaluate an employee for the purpose of gathering information with which to "hang" the employee, and the ethical psychiatrist should not agree to function in this role. Management's motives are usually constructive, even though the employee's perception about them may be quite different. Managers rarely request personal information that is not relevant to the job situation. If they do, it is the psychiatrist's job to draw lines clearly as to what information is appropriate to a manager's purpose.

Because the potential for conflict of interest remains, the occupational psychiatrist must always be vigilant. The best rule of thumb is that role ambiguities should be clarified *before* entering into a situation with a potential for conflict.

A working alliance must be formed with the individual, with the understanding that the consultant was hired by management. Resistances that could interfere with the consultation need to be worked through. Making the terms of confidentiality explicit, and acknowledging any real limits, can usually overcome the employee's natural feeling of mistrust and suspiciousness.

It may be helpful to see the employee in the psychiatrist's private office or in some place separate from the workplace. However, one must first ask: 1) is private office space available in the workplace for psychiatric interviews? 2) can the employee have the time off to leave the facility? and 3) will the employee feel it is a violation of his or her confidentiality to meet with the psychiatrist on the worksite in full view of others? The occupational psychiatrist must have sufficient knowledge of the organizational culture if he or she is to gain the cooperation of the individual in resolving the problem. Legal matters, financial issues, conflicts with management, or personal issues unrelated to the organization may be dealt with in the individual consultation.

In addition to the resistance of the individual managers and employees, union leadership—which traditionally "takes care of its own"—often raises major questions about the usefulness of management-sponsored mental health services. Union leaders frequently fear that these programs will make the employees more compliant to the wishes of management. Union representatives are also concerned that mental health services can undermine the grievance procedure by discrediting an employee on psychiatric grounds. This resistance can be reduced by involving the union in planning and sponsoring psychiatric consultation services.

Furthermore, the occupational psychiatrist, serving as an outside consultant, might pose a threat to the full-time Medical Department at a company. He or she may be perceived as being aligned with management, privy to certain important sources of information, and not being part of the medical team. Often this is in fact true, because the nature of the original contract generally comes directly through management rather than from the Medical Department.

Interestingly, some of the most important obstacles to functioning in the workplace arise from within the psychiatrist him- or herself—particularly the interference of unresolved conflicts around issues of power, authority, control, aggression, exhibitionism, and money. Most industrial settings distribute power and authority in a hierarchical fashion. Each employee reports to a supervisor who assumes responsibility for the overall quality of the individual's work. Although the concepts of worker democracy and participatory management have been introduced into the workplace during the last 15 or 20 years, the vast majority of workplaces continue to have relatively rigid authority structures that employ a variety of more or less coercive techniques to gain employee cooperation. However, the hierarchical structures serve the vital functions of distributing information effectively and aiding in the creation and coordination of activities. Psychiatrists must manage their own possibly irrational feelings toward authority and hierarchical institutions. They may find themselves subtly censured by psychiatric colleagues for being too identified with more action-oriented, aggressive managers.

It is not uncommon for individuals who have sought medicine and psychiatry as professions to have been motivated, at least in part, by conscious and unconscious desires to avoid becoming enmeshed in rigid and authoritarian structures. If they have a more academic bent, they will more likely tolerate a university's hierarchic structure than the bottom-line orientation of an industrial organization. Economic constraints can seem contrary to humanistic ideals. Sometimes they are; but they do not necessarily have to be—and that is where the occupational psychiatrist can fit in.

Working as a psychiatric consultant in an occupational setting can revive unresolved conflicts about competition, rivalry, dominance, submission, and rebellion. Managers feel extremely comfortable talking about "more aggressive penetration of customers" or "competitive strategy." The symbolic meaning of those statements is helpful to the psychiatrist in developing an intervention strategy. But psychoanalytic interpretations are for the psychiatrist's own understanding. Such concepts need to be translated for the organization using either appropriate corporate terminology or jargon-free expressions.

A psychiatrist's feelings of resentment, moral superiority, and even unconscious feelings of envy (e.g., regarding salary, stock options, benefits, etc.) can lead him or her to act out conflicts with the organization in inappropriate ways. Countertransference can emerge toward an institution as well as toward an individual or small group, but defining the feelings as countertransferences may be new for most psychiatrists. For example, one newly initiated occupational psychiatrist, who was evaluating a senior member of management for a Fortune 500 firm for depression, elicited the history that the executive's depression appeared to be precipitated by the knowledge that his annual bonus would be reduced from $2 million to $1 million. The psychiatrist unwittingly made the remark: "One million dollars appears to be more than enough." The core issue is the experience and meaning of the event to the individual, not for the psychiatrist to determine the merit or equity of the compensation. Such a response is a countertransference being acted out.

Although prejudice against rich people can be tempting to a psychiatrist, it is prejudice nonetheless and just as destructive as prejudice toward poor people. From a broader perspective, the psychiatrist's unresolved countertransference issues alienate the individual and preclude the opportunity of establishing a meaningful therapeutic alliance. The implications are far beyond the dyadic relationship. An influential corporate person may have a major impact on policy making regarding the place of mental health within the organization.

The occupational psychiatrist commonly feels an initial sense of inadequacy and ignorance. Very few psychiatrists during their training have been exposed to this field, either from a didactic or a clinical point of view. Occupational psychiatry focuses on the interplay of forces, not only at the intrapsychic and interpersonal levels, but also at the organizational, political, and societal levels.

Until very recently, academic psychiatry has been uninterested in the problems of the workplace. Consequently, many occupational psychiatrists who are qualified to teach often find themselves out of step with the theoretical orientation and pragmatic goals of academic departments. This can leave occupational psychiatrists with the problem of identity diffusion and hungry for professional support and collegial bonds. Although these psychiatrists try to support others in lonely positions (e.g., chief executive officers), they also need to find allies and friends for themselves.

Another frustration is that appropriate workplace literature is difficult to collect, because problems of the workplace cut across the fields of sociology, social and industrial psychology, anthropology, organizational behavior, and personnel management. It is often difficult to get a sense of what is important to read or study. Comprehensive overviews of the field are rare.

Lack of exposure to the problems of the workplace is further aggravated by a paucity of colleagues who practice in the workplace. With the exception of the APA Task Force on Occupational Psychiatry, the GAP Committee on Psychiatry in Industry, and the Academy of Occupational and Organizational Psychiatry, there are few high-quality continuing education programs available to acquaint the clinical psychiatrist in practice with the problems of the workplace. There is much more available to psychologists who choose to work on such problems.

As a result of the above-mentioned obstacles, it is not uncommon for the psychiatrist who entertains the idea of involvement in the workplace to feel overwhelmed, insecure, and inadequate. Those who decide to take on the challenge have to work through a sense of impotence. They will have less control over certain aspects of their work than they did before, and measurement of success and failure will be more unclear (e.g., when compared with biological psychiatry).

Once one has secured a position within the occupational setting, there are other obstacles to overcome. Often the occupational psychiatrist is involved in a wide variety of professional activities in the workplace. Given the needs of the individual clients and organization, one can find oneself involved in crisis intervention, brief psychotherapy, career counseling, marital therapy, diagnosis and referral, medication evaluation, organizational consultation, and consulting with senior management. The psychiatrist can feel pulled apart. Some feelings of anxiety are normal.

On a number of different occasions, for example, one may need to see a psychotic employee who needs immediate hospitalization; evaluate a depressed secretary for medication; counsel an irate worker about how to get along with a supervisor; convince a vice president who is abusing alcohol to seek treatment; give a seminar to management about a troubled employee; and consult with the CEO about a new organizational structure for a division.

Given the great diversity of tasks that one may be asked to do, the inexperienced psychiatrist may feel overwhelmed, unskilled, and fatigued. With travel to satellite offices for clinical consultations and trouble-shooting plant tours, he or she can feel physically drained as well. This may lead to reactions of avoidance and denial.

3

Pathways Into Occupational Psychiatry

Every man's work is a portrait of himself.

Samuel Butler
The Way of All Flesh

Because there have been no formal training programs in occupational psychiatry, colleagues frequently ask how they can become involved in this specialty. An opportunity to consult to an organization may be a serendipitous or planned experience. We may meet someone at a social occasion who is intrigued by what a psychiatrist might be able to do in his or her work environment. We may know a supervisor working in an organization who needs additional assistance. We may hear about an unexpected opening for a consultant, or "cold call" a number of organizations in town to determine whether they can use the assistance of a psychiatrist.

The purpose of this chapter is to acquaint psychiatric residents and other interested psychiatrists with the ways that several occupational psychiatrists entered this field and developed their careers in it. We are presenting highly personalized accounts of eight occupational psychiatrists who contributed to the writing of this report. Because of the mentoring value that these might have, they are consequently written in the first person. We hope that this chapter will provide an in-depth sense of the professional development of a few individuals, and we believe this to be more helpful than a comprehensive listing of pathways into occupational psychiatry. As psychiatrists interested in the inner dynamics of work and career development, we understand the crucial importance of mentoring and identification in that process.

It is important to reiterate that these examples of occupational psychiatrists highlight the corporate setting, because historically, that is where this field has been located. As we stated in the introduction to this book, military, prison, government, college, and union psychiatrists can legitimately be called "occupational" psychiatrists, because they all function in workplace settings; but they have organized themselves separately and under different names.

A Psychiatric Consultant to a Computer Company

While serving as a psychiatric chief resident, I met an experienced corporate psychiatric consultant. He had served as an advisor to a major computer company and had established a Center for Occupational Mental Health. The center sponsored several international meetings on work stress and compiled a newsletter dealing with occupational psychiatry. My relationship with him as well as the presence of this center facilitated my exploration of the occupational psychiatry literature, which included articles in occupational medicine, social psychology, anthropology, sociology, and physiology.

After completing my residency, I was invited to serve as psychiatric consultant to the regional medical department of the large computer manufacturing and marketing company where my former mentor worked. Initially my primary responsibilities consisted of clinical evaluation, referral for treatment, liaison with treating physicians and therapists, and monitoring of chronic psychiatric problems among the employees.

Patients were referred for psychiatric evaluation by occupational physicians and nurses, managers, and personnel specialists. At least half of all patients seen were self-referred. As I gained experience and earned trust, I was asked to participate in personnel meetings focusing on troubled employees and on Corporate Disability Adjudication Panels. In addition, I taught management seminars on stress, substance abuse, and workplace violence.

Participation in local occupational medical meetings facilitated relationships with medical directors of other companies. I became a part-time consultant to two major utilities and a school district. With a sense of growing expertise from my experience and my academic study, I extended my consultation practice to worker's compensation hearings, disability panels, and liability litigation. I also taught at a medical school at the undergraduate and graduate levels and wrote articles on the troubled worker, fitness for work evaluations, and disproportionate disability. A deepening appreciation of the complex problems in delivering and funding adequate psychiatric care led to graduate studies culminating in a master's degree in public health.

In my private practice, I have enriched psychoanalytically oriented psychotherapy with a deeper understanding of social issues, including the dynamics of the workplace. Psychiatric consultation to industry led me to more profound insights regarding identity development, transference, and interpersonal relationships.

A Researcher of Leadership

I graduated from medical school in 1974, completed my psychiatric residency in 1978, and received a master's degree in business administration (MBA) in 1979. My inspiration for this combined professional commitment developed after an initial interest in hospital management. Following my experience at business school, I began to focus on the psychology of executives. I continued my studies at the doctoral level in organizational development and subsequently served as a Special Assistant to the Secretary of Health and Human Services in Washington, DC, between 1979 and 1981. I also began psychoanalytic training during this period and completed it in 1988.

From 1982 to 1987, I directed a private psychiatric group practice, specializing in the psychological problems of employers and employees. The practice's clients included managers and employees of many large industrial corporations as well as federal government agencies.

In 1989, I again brought my varied interests and skills together—this time around the issue of leadership—by conceiving, developing, and running a research project on leadership under the aegis of the Department of Psychiatry of a local medical school. I brought together a group of scholars, clinicians, and leaders of business and government to develop a fundamental and unique body of knowledge about the leadership process. It emphasizes the complex interplay of individual behaviors and psychological dynamics that enhance or distort the leadership role. The research project distributes its pertinent research findings to lay leaders of public and private institutions through newsletters, journal articles, symposia, books, and media presentations.

In 1989 I wrote a book that is a primer on the impaired executive. It brings together my background in psychoanalysis and management and analyzes the executive from the intrapsychic and organizational levels. That year I also began a management consulting firm that assists senior executives in learning how to lead the emerging diverse work force of the 1990s—a work force that includes increasingly greater concentrations of women, African Americans, Hispanics, Asian Americans, and immigrants. I believe that the challenge to industry is to identify and modify those human resources management practices of selection, recruitment, development, retention, and promotion that will enhance the performance of this new group of employees. My management consulting firm analyzes and recommends changes in the corporate culture and organizational practices that may unknowingly inhibit the commitment, loyalty, and motivation of this new work force.

A Private Practitioner in a Business District

I became interested in occupational psychiatry as a resident, through a supervisor who was a part-time clinical consultant to two corporations. I completed my training in 1971. After being in practice and teaching psychiatry for several years, the germ of the supervisor's inspiration flourished into a mature interest, and I began to explore the possibility of working as a psychiatrist to a company myself. I was urged by my supervisor to call any large bank's medical director (I called the one at which I had an account), tell him or her of my interest, try to arrange a meeting, and ask for a job. The first Medical Director I called invited me to lunch at the bank's headquarters and did not offer me a job, but he did suggest that I develop a practice in the area where banks, brokerage, insurance, and legal firms were located and where more than half a million people came to work each day. These firms, in 1975, had a great need for an accessible psychiatric consultant.

Within 3 months, I had rented office space there; and before a year was up I was practicing exclusively in the community. I met with the medical people who worked there, joined local groups of occupational physicians, was invited to give talks to various business and professional groups about psychological stressors in the workplace and what to do about them, and joined the staff of a small community hospital in the area to teach psychiatry to the medical house staff. Referrals came to my practice from all levels—top executives to clerical workers. I was asked to consult in psychiatric emergencies that arose in the workplace and made treatment and referral recommendations.

One clinical challenge that I faced became the inspiration for a book I wrote that was published in 1980. Many of my most occupationally successful patients seemed addicted to their work and often unable to function satisfactorily in personal relationships that were not goal-directed. Their home lives were often chaotic and filled with anger, frustration, and conflict. They complained of emptiness whenever they were away from work.

My book explored the discrete psychologies of working and loving and the complex dynamics of the syndrome of "workaholism." This led to ongoing research into the normal and pathological interaction between career and home, and to frequent requests for me to speak before various groups on issues such as midlife crisis, two-career families, pathological ambition, "money addiction," and so on. Referrals to my practice continue to come heavily from sources in the workplace where debilitating intrapsychic conflict may first manifest itself, or where there may be a greater willingness to confront pathology than at home.

By virtue of my locating my office where my patients work, people often come to me for treatment with the expectation that I will understand and speak the language of their business—which, for many of my patients, is what their sense of self primarily rests on. Work-related fantasies and conflicts do provide a rich opportunity for investigating intrapsychic processes. I have also found that detailed inquiries into the specifics of the financial facts of my patients' lives (both in taking an initial history and during the course of therapy) can lead to significant insights into highly sensitive subconscious material.

A Psychiatrist at a Medical Center

I developed an interest in occupational psychiatry while I was a Fellow in college mental health. At that time, I was asked to serve as psychiatric consultant to India 21, a Peace Corps training project involving faculty from medical and business schools. As part of the India 21 project, volunteers were trained to consult to small businesses in India to improve productivity. In the course of this consultative service, I found that concepts of psychotherapy and life-cycle issues had many effective applications in the world of work.

This fellowship helped prepare me for a full-time occupational psychiatry position in the federal government in Washington, DC. I was hired to organize a psychiatric consultation and education service that provided part-time psychiatrists for 10 governmental agencies. The program offered telephone consultations regarding troubled employees; education and training of physicians and nurses with respect to doctor-patient relationships, suicide, alcoholism, homosexuality, retirement, and other frequently encountered topics; and mental health training for administrators, to assist them in resolving administrative problems with employees. The program that I began in 1967 is still in operation.

In 1969, I accepted a faculty position at a medical school in the Midwest as a National Institute of Mental Health (NIMH) Career

Teacher in Psychiatry. In addition to my teaching responsibilities, I served as a part-time consultant to a large manufacturer of corrugated boxes. As an industrial psychiatrist, I provided consultation to plant employees and taught management programs to the production staff and sales force to improve interpersonal relationships and productivity in the workplace.

In 1971, I began my tenure as Chairman of the Department of Psychiatry at a local medical center, where I also maintain a private psychiatric practice. My interests in occupational psychiatry are presently best illustrated by my involvement in providing psychiatric consultations to various companies regarding disability, workers' compensation, and executive stress issues. I have coauthored a book with two colleagues on the subject of job loss, as I have a strong interest in exploring the relationship between job loss and physical and mental illness. My professional experiences combined with this research have strengthened my philosophy that work issues need to be emphasized more in psychiatric training and practice.

A Psychiatric Employee Assistance Program (EAP) Leader

During my psychiatric residency, I became very interested in the role of the work environment as a cause of psychiatric illness. In 1977, after attending business school, I established a nonprofit university-affiliated organization structured to investigate the impact of work on individuals and to develop methods of intervention for individual and organizational conflict. An interest in family therapy had shown me that individual pathology could be altered by intervention at the level of organization interaction.

When I entered the field of organizational psychiatry, I found I had many difficulties and feelings to face. First, many of my colleagues were critical of my decision. They either thought I was strange because of my interest in business or that I had "sold out." I found the business environment confusing. Much of the vocabulary was novel, the problems seemed enormous, and standards of acceptable behavior were rather restrictive. I alternated between a sense of smugness about my deeper understanding of motivation of behavior and a sense of inadequacy about how to apply this knowledge usefully. Periodically I would present projects to managers that seemed humanely urgent but that would be rejected out of hand. Lastly, I had to overcome a natural shyness about speaking to groups.

By 1984, the number of clients seeking my services grew beyond the university's capacity to handle them, and my center split off to become a for-profit institution. This consulting firm has 45 full-time employees, of whom 3 are psychiatrists. It also has contractual relationships with 1,500 people, of whom 200 are psychiatrists, and a roster of 100 corporate and governmental clients. It has three divisions: 1) organizational, 2) clinical, and 3) research. The organizational division consults to institutions on issues of long-term policy as they affect individuals and helps bring understanding of individual and group psychology to bear on effecting long-term constructive changes within the organization.

Organizational work begins with my consultations with a company's Chairman, President, and top management team. They use my psychiatric knowledge to alter organizational cultures in desired ways. This is the primary prevention arm of my firm. Structuring the internal environment of the organization to fit better with individual needs allows people to perform more successfully and to feel better. Further, these individuals become more psychologically minded, invested in interpersonal relationships, and flexible in their adaptational style. This results in a more healthy and profitable organization. Job loss is minimized, and there are more opportunities for advancement, professional development, and compensation.

The firm's clinical arm is its EAP. It trains supervisors in early detection of mental disturbance and substance abuse, publicizes self-referral for employees, and provides treatment and referral. The need for these programs has led to this becoming the largest psychiatrically-run EAP in the United States.

One issue quickly recognized when operating an EAP is the poor fit that often exists among psychiatric efforts, substance abuse problems, and insurance coverage to pay for these efforts. Often, treatment is shaped by benefits instead of benefits fitting the individual problem. By combining authorization of specific insurance coverage on a case-by-case basis with an EAP, it is possible to have payment fit the problem rather than vice versa. Employees are encouraged by their insurance benefits to contact their EAP. The program will recertify them for treatment and determine coverage on a case-by-case basis. The psychiatrist within the program can even move dollars between inpatient coverage to residential, partial day, and outpatient coverage as needed. This approach allows the company to contain costs and increase quality of care for its employees.

Finally, the research division of my firm develops new knowledge and products in the hope of advancing the field of occupational mental health. It also supports the efforts of the other two divisions. Currently, it is involved in a variety of research efforts, some federally funded and some underwritten through internal research and development allocations. For example, the division has developed a prototype of a computer tracking program to assess the progress of individual patients in outpatient psychotherapy and to help determine which therapists are most effective with their patients. The division has also established a self-report method to measure drug and alcohol use in employees. This procedure is supported by government funds and uses a new form of statistical validation to maximize reliability. Through this tool, organizations can determine the need for substance abuse programs. Furthermore, it can be used to spot areas within the organization with high substance use. In addition, the firm has just initiated a 5-year follow-up study to determine the criteria for deciding the type of treatment alcoholic patients should receive—outpatient, inpatient, psychiatric, or rehabilitation.

A Psychiatrist at a Business School

In 1967, while pursuing my interests in treatment issues for patients in late adolescence and early adulthood, I accepted a Fellowship in College Psychiatry. Toward the end of the program, my chief asked me to explore a potential new role as Psychiatrist for the business school at the university. I visited the school, studied its curriculum, and met with a number of faculty members and deans. After a number of consultations with trusted associates and a careful review of the prospects, I agreed to accept the position. This appointment represented a major shift in my professional interests. It was associated with a high degree of anxiety; but the prospects of exploring new arenas in psychiatry excited me.

My first year at the business school involved familiarizing myself with the environment, learning the culture and a new language, and being available to students, faculty, administrators, and other employees. Initially I experienced a number of problems—loneliness, ambivalence regarding my participation at the school, alienation from colleagues, and a need to overcome a resistance on the part of faculty who had difficulty understanding my specific role at the school. During the first year, I initiated a series of meetings with deans, department heads, members of the dietary and library services, and a number of student groups. I considered it important to visit them on their own turf, explore the issues, and then design programs to deal with these needs. It became increasingly evident that my effectiveness would, to a large extent, be determined by understanding the customs, rituals, and language of the environment, as well as the ability to be trusted by various groups—and to add value to an already rich curriculum.

The student body consisted of approximately 1,500 MBA candidates. I was available to these students for consultation and treatment. Some sought me out to resolve conflicts in their lives over issues such as power and authority. Others experienced major conflicts reinforced by the competitive and demanding environment of the business school. Still others had serious psychiatric symptoms, including anxiety, depression, character disorders (primarily narcissistic), and psychophysiological and sexual disturbances. A minority (less than 1%) of students required hospitalization.

Particularly impressive was the stress manifested by married students in the MBA program. Many experienced concern over possible effects that the school's demanding program would impose on their relationships with their spouses. Spouses initially felt angry, jealous, rejected, and consumed with guilt or rage as they realized the compromises they were expected to make for the sake of a husband's or wife's career. Some harbored the fantasy that life would change significantly for the better after graduation; it would be more controlled and hence less stressful. Others perceived that the shift from school to job would produce positive change only if they actively thought about priorities in their lives, established them early, and acted upon them. Some of these couples were seen together, others in group therapy.

After about a year at the school, I met with the academic deans and received permission to establish a second-year elective (for credit) on the executive family. The seminar had a number of specific goals:

- To focus on the conflicts of business school couples;
- To anticipate the interrelationships of individuals, families, and business organizations following graduation;
- To help husband and wife recognize that successful marriages and careers would depend on creative work by both parties;
- To explore the trade-offs each couple would make as they became more intimately involved in planning their interpersonal and professional lives; and
- To concentrate on "normal" development of talented, aggressive, and perceptive couples engaged in the business world rather than to focus on psychopathology.

The seminar consisted of 16 weekly classes. It included specific topics such as dual careers, work philosophies, dynamics of business travel and job relocation, problems of success, impact of job loss on individuals and families, executive families living abroad, and changing roles of men and women in the business world. As a direct outgrowth of this seminar, I coauthored a book about the dynamic interrelationship of the executive with his or her family and work organizations.

In 1984, I left the business school and established The Center for the Study of Work at a psychiatric hospital. The program provided consultation to industry as well as conferences and seminars and had training and research components. I continue to consult and lecture to a wide range of organizations. Most recently, I coauthored a book dealing with the psychosocial impact of job loss. Consultation in the workplace has given me the opportunity to work with diverse groups and to apply psychodynamic principles in a unique way.

An Executive Consultant

I developed an interest in preventive psychiatry during my residency. This was initially stimulated by a seminar given for executives and occupational physicians in the hospital's division of industrial mental health. Central to the course was the notion that good management practices and good health practices were usually the same, and that emotional harm to workers comes as much from trying to be too kind to them as from being uncaring. From this experience, I found that I enjoyed working in the occupational arena. While I was still a resident and after I became a staff psychiatrist, I performed consultations for organizations that requested help with issues including prejudice in the workplace, participatory management, prolonged layoffs, and people-oriented management development. The executives I worked with asked for time to talk openly about all aspects of their own lives, personal as well as business. These were by and large healthy people who wanted a chance to tie together emotionally charged issues from within their own personal histories, their families, and their workplaces.

Because many of these executives were coming from other parts of the country and because their needs were complex, I developed the structure for a daylong executive consultation. I designed a methodology for this "executive mental health exam." It was at this point that I founded a private consulting firm and marketed its services to domestic and foreign corporations.

The "Executive Consultation" attempts to combine psychiatric and business insights into the individual's life. My firm sends an extensive questionnaire to a prospective consultee that he or she completes prior to the visit. On arrival, the executive, sometimes accompanied by his or her spouse, has 2 hours of psychological testing and personality surveys administered by a clinical psychologist. He or she also spends 2 to 3 hours with a psychiatrist in a general clinical interview, and then 1 hour with a management consultant. The final step consists of 1 to 2 hours of feedback and recommendations with the whole consultation team.

The executive consultation goes beyond giving the client a clean bill of health or a diagnosis and referral for treatment. Ideally, it tells the executive who he or she is, and how his or her personality affects management style and personal relationships. It identifies trouble spots. Over lunch, the consultants review the morning's information and summarize the person's strengths and weaknesses organized under "personal," "organizational," and "family" issues. The executive receives a typed version of these during the feedback session. This brief includes the most important personal issues for the executive to address in the next 6 to 12 months.

My firm has now completed nearly 600 executive consultations. It also provides comprehensive assistance to people whose positions are in jeopardy in the organization or who are identified as sources of trouble. The person and his or her boss, peers, and subordinates are interviewed, and a plan is devised for the company to make changes to enhance individual-organizational fit. Follow-up services by professionals are then provided to support the change process.

As an occupational psychiatrist, I have been the psychiatric consultant to a major U.S. city, three federal agencies, a bank dealing with the aftermath of an earthquake, and a support group for city managers. The dynamic interaction between good management and good health continues to serve as a foundation of my practice. I have had a professional relationship with many of my corporate clients for over 15 years.

Founder of a Center for Work and Mental Health

After spending a few years in a traditional private-practice model of psychiatry, I took the step of forming an outpatient mental health group located in a metropolitan financial district. Our center has been providing a range of services that has utilized psychologists and psychiatrists since 1985. Although traditional individual psychotherapy takes place, the center's staff also provide other services not commonly taught in residency training. We perform psychiatric evaluations and provide reports on medicolegal issues such as fitness for duty, long-term disability, and workers' compensation benefits. Employees referred for such forensic examinations include police officers involved in shootings, bank tellers who have been robbed, construction workers with chronic pain syndromes, painters with solvent exposure, and teachers struggling with large classes in an urban setting. There are a myriad of other clinical presentations involving individuals in a variety of professional paths who find themselves experiencing psychiatric symptoms that affect their capacity to work. One of the important functions that clinicians provide at the center is helping other professionals (e.g., claims examiners or administrative law judges, to make decisions about benefit provision). The doctors at the center have had to learn a new language involving terms such as apportionment of responsibility, work function impairment, and eligibility for vocational rehabilitation.

Referrals come to the center from other doctors, but primarily from insurance carrier representatives, plaintiff and defense attorneys, EAPs, human resource departments, and the state department overseeing workers' compensation. When referrals do come from clinicians, they often involve questions from occupational physicians or toxicologists. The center provides educational services not only to employee groups through noontime lectures, but also through in-service training to non-clinical professionals. I have participated in educational programs for attorneys, insurers, and occupational medicine clinicians. I have served as president of the state's occupational medicine association.

Another role that I have enjoyed in the association has been that of the educational program chairman for a number of meetings. Topics discussed have included the automated work station, women in the work force, multiple chemical sensitivities, and optimal training and prevention of injuries in professional athletes. In my role as an officer for the medical association, I have testified before the state legislature on a number of occasions concerning pending bills related to workers' compensation and safety issues. Currently I am a member of a 14-doctor panel overseeing health care services within the state's $10 billion annual budget for its workers' compensation system.

My faculty appointment is within the Department of Psychiatry at the local university, although I teach primarily through the Division of Occupational and Environmental Medicine. I have helped to cochair university-sponsored national meetings on the subject of work and mental health. Still, my primary professional commitment is through the center. Over time, that outpatient mental health group has continued to evolve. The center now provides a reference service to its referral sources producing annotated bibliographies on a variety of subjects such as posttraumatic stress and disability. Timely articles that appear in publications such as the *Journal of Occupational Medicine* on subjects such as somatoform presentations are summarized and then distributed to referral sources. With time, my goal is to provide prevention and early intervention based on a public health model for physical and mental injuries in the workplace.

Aside from my clinical and administrative roles, I am also interested in education. My current areas of interest in my writings include ethics in the occupational medicine field. I recently coedited a book on psychiatric injuries in the workplace.

4

Guidelines for the Occupational Psychiatrist

Let us work without questioning; it is the only way to make life tolerable.

Voltaire
Candide

1. Advocate Biopsychosocial Health

The occupational psychiatrist is primarily concerned with the proper functioning of the individual and the organization in the world of work. He or she is an advocate for health. Consequently, his or her actions must contribute to environmental changes that support mental health. This approach answers the question, "Is the occupational psychiatrist just a 'tool of management'?"

2. Understand the "Psychological Contract"

The occupational psychiatrist must be mindful that there may be a "psychological contract" between the employees and the employer in addition to any written employment contract. Not uncommonly, this includes the employee's expectations with regard to loyalty, caretaking, and so on by the corporation.

3. Maintain Confidentiality

The maintenance of confidentiality is critical. Where the extent of confidentiality is limited, it must be disclosed to the employee before obtaining information. Gaining a reputation as a source of "leaks" can severely inhibit the occupational psychiatrist's chances of success in a company.

4. Get Supervision

Adequate supervision by seasoned colleagues with experience in occupational consultations during the occupational psychiatrist's initial organizational experiences is extraordinarily useful in gaining needed perspective on the dynamics of the organization. Names of such colleagues are available through the APA Task Force on Occupational Psychiatry, the GAP Committee on Psychiatry in Industry, and the American Association of Occupational and Organizational Psychiatrists. In addition, selected publications in specific areas can be most helpful in this matter.

5. Review the Literature

The occupational psychiatrist must periodically review the literature of occupational psychiatry and related field. Study groups with interested colleagues in allied fields can be most helpful.

6. Explore Transference and Countertransference

The occupational psychiatrist must periodically explore transference and countertransference issues regarding work and power. Unresolved conflicts involving envy, jealousy, and competitiveness can lead to undue aggressiveness or passivity in the work setting. He or she should seek therapy or analysis if necessary.

7. Understand All the Components of the Organization

It is of utmost importance to understand the history, goals, conflicts, and problem-solving methods of the organization.

8. Be Available at All Organizational Levels

The occupational psychiatrist should make him- or herself available at all levels in the organization so as to become familiar with the different issues as well as to gain trust. The more the occupational psychiatrist knows about the setting and its participants, the better he or she will understand the formal and informal use of power.

9. Establish Realistic Goals

Goals should be realistic. The occupational psychiatrist should not overextend him- or herself and make unrealistic promises. He or she should avoid consulting to senior management about broad organizational issues until he or she has substantial experience. Inappropriate grandiosity on the part of the consultant in the beginning can quickly lead to failure and disappointment for all parties.

10. Move Slowly

It is important for the occupational psychiatrist to get his or her feet wet slowly. He or she must commit increasing amounts of time and energy to the occupational setting only as confidence, experience, and time commitment allow, to avoid premature failure and feelings of inadequacy and frustration.

11. Communicate Clearly and Without Jargon

Consultation and communication at all levels in the organization should be clear, concise, and jargon-free. Using obscure and unfamiliar psychiatric terminology alienates more individuals than it serves. When speaking to managers about personnel issues, the occupational psychiatrist should avoid phrases such as "negative transference," "unresolved Oedipal-level conflicts," and the like.

12. Recognize Individual Versus Organizational Trade-offs

Any recommendations or advice offered must take into account the essential and difficult trade-offs between the individual and the organization. What is good for the individual is not always necessarily good for the organization, and vice versa.

13. Know Your Role

The occupational psychiatrist should avoid slipping into a quasi-managerial role by assuming certain staff or line functions that are the proper responsibility of the organization's executives. He or she should avoid giving executives advice about devising long-range strategic plans, developing new marketing strategies, and increasing manufacturing productivity. The psychiatrist is a consultant—not an executive.

14. Make Use of a Team Approach

The occupational psychiatrist should take a cooperative team approach to organizational consultation. Participants in the organization who are invited to become part of the solution are less likely to remain part of the problem. It is necessary to get executives, line managers, and employees involved in helping solve difficult problems.

15. Avoid Conflict of Interest

The occupational psychiatrist must avoid conflict of interest. He or she should not be a consultant to, as well as a significant shareholder in, the organization and must not see employees or executives in private practice and consult with them in the organization. Where a case involves legal or administrative issues, the psychiatrist cannot be both the treating physician and an independent examiner.

16. Be Clinically Flexible

The occupational psychiatrist must consider various treatment options and means of intervention. Although in certain instances a focus on the individual through psychotherapy, medication, or behavioral approaches may be sufficient, in others a systems approach making recommendations for the larger work group will be most effective.

17. Know Your Limitations

The occupational psychiatrist should always maintain a healthy respect for the limitations of his or her ability to change fundamental systems within the organization. Organizations change slowly.

Afterword

And the end of all our exploring
will be to arrive where we started
and know the place for the first time.

T. S. Eliot
"Little Gidding"
The Four Quartets

The emerging issues that business and industry will be forced to face in the next decade will offer significant challenges and opportunities in the field of occupational psychiatry. As *Work Force 2000: Work and Workers of the 21st Century* (Johnston and Packer 1987) states:

> The last years of this century are certain to bring new developments in technology, international competition, demography, and other factors that will alter the nation's economic and social landscape. By the end of the next decade, the changes under way will produce an America that is in some ways unrecognizable from the one that existed only a few years ago. Four key trends will shape the last years of the 20th century. (p. xiii)
>
> I. The American economy should grow at a relatively healthy pace, boosted by a rebound of U.S. exports, renewed productivity, and a strong world economy.
>
> II. Despite its international comeback, U.S. manufacturing may be a much smaller share of the economy in the year 2000 than it is today. Service industries will create most of the new jobs and most of the new wealth in the next decade.
>
> III. The work force will grow slowly, with more workers who are older, female, or disadvantaged. Only 15% of new entrants in the labor force over the next 13 years will be white American-born males, compared with 47% in that category today.
>
> IV. The new jobs in service industries will demand much higher skills than the jobs today. Ironically, the demographic trends in the work force coupled with the highest skill requirements of the economy will lead to both higher and lower unemployment: more jobless-

ness among the least skilled and less among the most educationally advantaged.

The predictions indicate a future work world subject to enormous change, uncertainty, and pressure. This will require a comprehensive understanding of the history, goals, and values of members of each group as they attempt to establish a legitimate identity in the work force. Psychiatrists, along with other social scientists, will have the opportunity to consult to organizations on a number of critical issues. Such opportunities include the following:

- Managing conflict of diverse groups (e.g., African Americans, Hispanics, and immigrants).
- Developing strategies to deal with job insecurity and the impact of unemployment (Group for the Advancement of Psychiatry 1982; Kates et al. 1990) as a result of competition, technology, mergers and acquisitions, plant closings, leveraged buyouts, and industry obsolescence.
- Maintaining productivity of an increasingly less skilled and shrinking entry-level work force.
- Monitoring the impact of mental health and morale on productivity.
- Providing guidelines for organizations as they undergo rapid change as a result of restructuring and downsizing.
- Establishing programs dealing with the recognition and treatment of substance abuse, alcoholism, and AIDS.
- Working with psychiatric colleagues and others in allied mental health fields in defining and redefining diagnostic categories in the workplace.
- Establishing short-term treatment programs to minimize "lost time" in the workplace.
- Consulting the government, insurance companies, and HMOs on specific benefit programs.
- Assessing psychiatric disability, work impairment, and fitness for duty.
- Jointly working with outplacement organizations with regard to career transitions.
- Introducing an occupational psychiatry elective in psychiatric residency programs, with the eventual development of an Occupational Psychiatry Fellowship.
- Developing a national clearinghouse to provide a data base for occupational psychiatry literature.
- Establishing a professional society (the American Organization of Occupational Psychiatrists [AOOP]).

Specialties of psychiatry and management have changed dramatically over the past several decades.

> The traditional or control-oriented approach to work force management took shape during the early part of the century. At the heart of this model was the wish to establish order, exercise control, and achieve efficiency in the application of the work force. This has given way to a *new commitment*, based on the approach to the work force in which jobs are designed to be broader than before and individual responsibilities are expected to change as conditions change, and where expertise rather than formal position determine influence. (Walton 1979, p. 88)

The members of the GAP Committee on Psychiatry in Industry genuinely believe that the occupational psychiatrist, because of his or her unique expertise, can make a significant difference in improving the productivity and self-esteem of the work force of the future.

Appendixes

The psychiatric work history as well as Levinson's (1972) organizational history are presented as a guide for the consulting psychiatrist. Clearly, they should not be used as a checklist; rather, they highlight critical issues of individuals in organizational life cycles.

Appendix A

Psychiatric Work History

Nature of the Job

Employer/job title

Tasks involved

Stresses
- 1) within the job
- 2) with peers
- 3) with superiors
- 4) with family life

Time in position

Hours worked and shifts

Opportunities for advancement

Control over work environment

Job Satisfaction

Meets career goals

Opportunities for using skills and interests

Congruent with self-esteem

Material benefits/pension

Previous thoughts of leaving

What individual would (could) change

Reinforces/undermines self-image

Work Career

Level of education and qualifications
Previous jobs
Reason(s) for leaving; duration of employment before leaving
Long-term plans
Promotions and demotions
Employment strengths and weaknesses

Financial Issues

Sources of income
Levels of income
Net worth, expenses, obligations

Previous Periods of Unemployment

Reasons
Duration
How ended
Problems encountered; how solved
Impact on self, relationships

Attitudes Toward Work

Attitudes toward working; attitudes toward not working
Spouse's attitude

Grievances

Compensation claims
Lawsuits

Work and Family

Demands of job on family life

Demands of working spouse
Overlap of work activities; relative importance
Support from family
Employment of parents/grandparents

Work and Family of Origin

Ethnic background and values
Parental jobs and their impact
Parental expectations and interest
Influences on career choice
Reasons for career choice
Thwarted aspirations

Personal Factors and Work

Authority figures
Autonomy
Dependency
Responsibility
Work habits
Relationship to others; expectations of others
Dealing with disappointment
Ability to anticipate and/or accommodate change
Power and competition

Medical and Psychiatric Disorders

Course of illness
Rehabilitation needs
Illness deficits
Work behaviors
Confidence

Periods of Disabilities or Substance Abuse

Work and Job-Finding Strengths

Skills and aptitudes
Resources
Knowledge of opportunities
Attitude
Contracts

Social Activities

Work-linked supports
Employee-linked supports
Time demands; overlap among them

Note: This table is a comprehensive list of areas to pursue when obtaining a psychiatric work history. Although not every question needs to be asked in each case, it is important to cover relevant areas in sufficient depth so that useful information can be elicited. Information can also be obtained on nonoccupational aspects of interpersonal or intrapsychic functioning, using work issues as a vehicle that will generate other material.
Source. Adapted from Kates et al. 1990, Table 5–1, pp 122–123. Used with permission.

Appendix B

Organizational History

Modification of Levinson's case study outline for organizations (1972, pp. 55–65)

I. GENETIC DATA
  A. Identifying Information
    1. Organization name
    2. Location
    3. Type of organization
    4. Organizational affiliation
    5. Size
    6. Situation of the initial contract
    7. Circumstances of the study
    8. Specific conditions affecting validity of the study
    9. First overall impressions
  B. Historical Data
    1. Chief complaint or events leading to the initiation of the study
    2. Problems of the organization as stated by key figures
      a. Long-range
      b. Short-range
    3. Background of the organization
      a. Key developmental phases
      b. Major crises experienced by the organization

c. Product-service history
d. Organizational folklore
4. Circumstances surrounding study

II. DESCRIPTION AND ANALYSIS OF CURRENT ORGANIZATION AS A WHOLE
A. Structural Data
1. Formal organization
a. Chart
b. Systems concept
c. Formal job description
2. Plant and equipment
3. Ecology of the organization
a. Spatial distribution of individuals
b. Spatial distribution of activities
c. Implications of the data on spatial distribution
4. Financial structure
5. Personnel
a. How many people are employed?
b. Where do they come from and what is their ethnic composition?
c. What are the various educational levels?
d. What is the average tenure?
e. What is the range of skills?
f. What is the absentee rate?
g. What is the turnover rate?
h. What is the accident rate?
6. Structure for handling personnel
a. Recruitment
b. Orientation
c. Training
d. Growth on the job
e. Promotion
f. Compensation
g. Performance analysis

h. Kind and intensity of supervision
i. Rules and regulations for employees
j. Medical program
k. Safety program
l. Retirement program
m. Recreation program
n. Other fringe benefits
o. Labor contract

7. Policies and procedures
   a. Scope
   b. How they are communicated
   c. Who knows about them
   d. What discretion is left to lower supervisory levels
8. Time span and rhythm
   a. Seasonal cycles
   b. Diurnal cycles
   c. Planning spans
   d. Degree activities are regulated by time
   e. Attitudes about punctuality
   f. Urgency
   g. Concern about deliveries

B. Process Data
   1. Communications systems
      a. Incoming: reception and routing
      b. Processing: integration, decision
      c. Outgoing: routing and response
   2. Current and previous studies in and reports to the organization

III. INTERPRETIVE DATA
   A. Current Organizational Functioning
      1. Organizational perceptions
         a. Degree of alertness, accuracy, and vividness
            (1) To stimuli from within the organization
               (A) From personnel

i. Employees to management and vice versa

ii. Supervisor to subordinate and vice versa

iii. Departments to each other's needs

b. Assessment of the discrepancy between reality and perceived reality

(1) Of reality within the organization

(2) Of reality outside the organization

2. Organizational knowledge

a. Acquisition of knowledge

(1) Methods of obtaining new knowledge

(2) Degree of receptivity to new knowledge

(3) Level and range of knowledge

b. Use of knowledge

(1) Flexibility

(2) Characteristic style and variations

c. Dissemination of knowledge

3. Organizational language

a. Themes and content of employee publications

b. Organizational ideology

c. Advertising themes

d. Organizational symbols and slogans

e. Language of policies as distinct from the policies themselves

f. Language of customs, taboos, prohibitions, and construction; direct and implied

4. Emotional atmosphere of the organization

a. Prevailing mood and range

b. Overall stability or variability of mood

c. Intraorganizational variability

(1) By hierarchical level

(2) By department

(3) Other (geographical location, profession)

5. Organizational action

a. Energy level

b. Qualities of action

B. Attitudes and Relationships
   1. Contemporary actions toward and relationships with others
      (1) Customers
      (2) Competition
      (3) Employees
      (4) Occupational associations and representatives
      (5) Stockholders
      (6) Legislative bodies
      (7) Executive and regulatory bodies (governmental)
      (8) Control bodies (internal)
      (9) Suppliers
      (10) Financial community
      (11) Host community
      (12) Dealer organizations
      (13) Plant builders
      (14) Consultants
      (15) Others
      a. Major attachments
      b. Masculine-feminine orientation
      c. Transference phenomena
         (1) Related to the consultant
         (2) Related to the organization
         (3) Related to each other
   2. Relations to things and ideas
      a. Quality and intensity of relations to plant, equipment, raw material or supplies, product and services
         (1) Symbolization
         (2) Unconscious personification
      b. Time: how is it regarded
         (1) Past, present, future orientation
         (2) How is future planned for
         (3) Is time valued as an investable commodity
         (4) View of work cycles
      c. Space: how is it conceptualized

(1) As a local concern
(2) As a cosmopolitan concern

d. Meaning of work for the organization
   (1) As a device for coping with the environment
      (A) In economic terms
      (B) In terms of skill
      (C) In terms of thinking
      (D) In terms of psychological defense
   (2) As a device for fulfilling psychological contract
   (3) As a device for channeling energy
      (A) Constructively
      (B) Destructively
      (C) As a process of regression
         i. Within the work setting
         ii. In non-work activities
e. Authority, power, and responsibility
   (1) How does the organization regard power
      (A) The power of others
      (B) Their own power vis-à-vis the world outside
      (C) Power internally
         i. Generally
         ii. By ranks
   (2) How does the organization handle authority
   (3) How does the organization handle responsibility
      (A) Outside the organization
      (B) Inside the organization
f. Positions on social, ethical, and political issues

3. Attitudes about self
   a. Who do they think they are and how do they feel about it
   b. Where do they think they are headed and how do they feel about it
   c. What are their common aspirations
   d. How do they look to themselves
4. Intraorganizational relationships

a. Key people in the organization
b. Significant groups within the organization
c. Implications of a and b

IV. ANALYSIS AND CONCLUSIONS
A. Organizational Integrative Patterns
1. Appraisal of the effect of the environment on the organization
a. Historical
b. Contemporary
c. Anticipated
(1) Beneficial
(2) Harmful
2. Appraisal of the effect of the organization on the environment
a. Historical
b. Contemporary
c. Anticipated
3. Reactions
a. Of the environment
(1) To the injury
(2) Toward source of the injury
b. Secondary reaction from the organization
4. Appraisal of the organization
a. Special assets
(A) REALITY ORIENTATION
i. To external environment
ii. To internal environment
(B) VALUES AND IDEALS
i. Degree of institutionalization
ii. Congruence with reality
(C) TASK MASTERY
i. Psychological contract fulfillment
ii. Growth and survival
iii. Task-directed behavior

b. Impairments
c. Level of integration
(1) Normal adaptive activities
(2) First-order adaptive activities
(3) Second-order adaptive activities
(4) Third- and fourth-order adaptive activities
d. Overall effectiveness and facade

B. Summary and Recommendations
1. Present status
2. Explanatory formulation
a. Genetic
b. Dynamic
3. Prognostic conclusions
4. Recommendations

Bibliography

Ament WW: Legal and ethical considerations in managing the troubled employee. Occupational Psychiatry: State of the Art Reviews 1(4):673–682, 1986

American Psychiatric Association, Committee on Occupational Psychiatry: Troubled People on the Job. Washington, DC, American Psychiatric Association, 1959

American Psychiatric Association, Committee on Occupational Psychiatry: The Mentally Ill Employee, His Treatment and Rehabilitation: A Guide for Management. New York, Harper & Row, 1965

American Psychiatric Association Council on National Affairs: Report of the Task Force on Psychiatry in Industry. Am J Psychiatry 141:1139–1144, 1984

American Psychiatric Association: Diagnostic and Statistical Manual of Mental Disorders, 3rd Edition, Revised. Washington, DC, American Psychiatric Association, 1987

Anderson VV: Psychiatry in Industry. New York, Harper, 1929

Argyris C: Understanding Organizational Behavior. New York, Dorsey, 1960

Becker CE, Larsen RC: Substance abuse and employee assistance programs, in Occupational Medicine. Edited by LaDou J. Norwalk, CT, Appleton & Lange, 1990

Bittker TE: The industrialization of American psychiatry. Am J Psychiatry 142(2):149–154, 1985

Blair BR: Selecting an EAP contractor that will meet company needs. Occup Health Saf 53(10):40–53, 1984

Brill P: Employee Assistance Programs: an overview and suggested roles for psychiatrists. Hosp Community Psychiatry 36:727–731, 1985

Brill PL, Hayes JO: Taming Your Turmoil: Managing the Transitions of Adult Life. Englewood Cliffs, NJ, Prentice-Hall, 1981

Broadbent DE: The clinical impact of job design. Br J Clin Psychol 24 (pt 1):33–40, 1985

Brodsky CM: The Harassed Worker. Lexington, MA, Lexington Books, 1976

Burling T: Training for industrial psychiatry. Am J Psychiatry 111:493–496, 1955
Burlingame CC: Psychiatry in industry. Am J Psychiatry 103:493, 1947a
Burlingame CC: Psychiatry in industry. Am J Psychiatry 103:549–553, 1947b
Carone P: Women in Industry. Albany, NY, State University of New York Press, South Oaks Foundation, 1977
Colligan MJ: An investigation of a case of apparent mass psychogenic illness in an electronics plant. J Behav Med 2(3):297–309, 1979
Collins RT: Industrial psychiatry. Am J Psychiatry 112:546, 1956
Committee on Psychiatry in Industry: The Application of Psychiatry to Industry (GAP Report No 20). New York, Group for the Advancement of Psychiatry, 1951
Cottington EM: Occupational stress, suppressed anger, and hypertension. Psychosom Med 48:249–260, 1986
Crull P: Stress effects of sexual harassment on the job. Am J Orthopsychiatry 52:539, 1982
Dickerson OB, Kaminer AJ: The Troubled Employee (State of the Art Reviews). Philadelphia, PA, Hanley & Belfus, October–December 1986
Dickman F: Employee Assistance Programs: basic concepts, attributes, and an evaluation. Personnel Administrator 27:55–58, 1982
Drucker PF: Management Task Responsibilities and Practices. New York, Harper & Row, 1973
Felton JS: Psychiatric orientation in the education of occupational physicians, in Occupational Psychiatry. Edited by Collins RT. International Psychiatric Clinics 6(4):123–139, 1969
Firth J: Burnout and professional depression: related concepts? J Adv Nurs 11(6):633–641, 1987
Firth-Cozens J: Emotional distress in junior house officers. BMJ 295(6597):533, 1987
Freud S: Civilization and Its Discontents (1930). Edited by Strachey J. New York, WW Norton, 1962
Gaeta E, Lynn R, Grey L: AT&T looks at program evaluation. EAP Digest 22(31), 1982
Ganster DC: Managing organizational stress: a field experiment. J Appl Psychol 67(5):533–542, 1982
Giannandrea PF: Psychodynamic approach to occupational psychiatry: comparative case studies. Am J Psychother 39(3):421–430, 1985
Giberson LG: Psychiatry in industry. Personnel Journal 15:90, 1936
Greiff BS: When an industrial plant closes. Boston Globe, 1973
Greiff BS: Psychiatry and the world of work. Psychiatric Opinion 15(12):10–18, 1978

Greiff BS, Munter PK: Tradeoffs: Executive Family and Organizational Life. New York, New American Library, 1980
Greiff S, Munter PK, Willig SH: Drug Abuse, Alcoholism and Their Effect on Business. Baltimore, MD, Dave Green Associates, 1970
Group for the Advancement of Psychiatry, Committee on Psychiatry in Industry: Job Loss: A Psychiatric Perspective. New York, Mental Health Materials Center, 1982
Hearle JM: The impact of EAP's on health insurance. EAP Digest 47(49), 1989
Hendrick I: The instinct to master. Psychoanal Q 12:516, 1943
Hennig M, Jardin A: The Managerial Woman. Garden City, NY, Anchor/Doubleday, 1977
Herzberg F: Work and the Nature of Man. Cleveland, OH, World Publishing Co, 1966
Hess H: Work in America: a psychiatric critique. J Occup Med 16(11), November 1974
Hirschfield A, Wagenheim H, Usher G: Interpersonal relations in industry (IRIS): a positive approach to industrial mental health. Am J Public Health 60(11):2094–2098, 1970
Hirschorn L: The Work Place Within: Psychodynamics of Organizational Life. Cambridge, MA, Massachusetts Institute of Technology Press, 1990
Hollman RW: Managing troubled employees: meeting the challenge. Journal of Contemporary Business 4:43–57, 1980
Huffman RE: Which soldiers break down: a survey of 610 psychiatric patients in Vietnam. Bull Menninger Clin 34(6):345, 1970
International Labour Organization: Encyclopedia of Occupational Health. New York, McGraw-Hill, 1972
Jacques E: The Changing Culture of a Factory. New York, Dryden, 1952
Johnston W, Packer A: Work Force 2000: Work and Workers for the 21st Century. New York, Hudson Institute, 1987
Jones KR: Impact of alcohol, drug abuse, and mental health treatment on medical care utilization. Med Care 17 (suppl):1–82, 1979
Kahn RL, et al: Report on stress in organizational settings, in Stress and Human Health. Edited by Elliott GR, Eisdorfer C. New York, Springer, 1982
Kanter RB: Men and Women of the Corporation. New York, Basic Books, 1977
Karasek R, Theorell T: Healthy Work: Stress, Productivity and the Reconstruction of Working Life. New York, Basic Books, 1990
Kates N, Greiff B, Hagen D: The Psychosocial Impact of Job Loss. Washington, DC, American Psychiatric Press, 1990

Kaufmann GM: Interactions between job stressors and social support: some counterintuitive results. J Appl Psychol 71(3):522–526, 1986
Krinsky L: Stress and Productivity, in Problems of Industrial Psychiatric Medicine, Vol 9. New York, Human Sciences Press, 1984
Lantos B: Work and the instincts. Int J Psychoanal 24:114–119, 1943
Lantos B: Metapsychological consideration on the concept of work. Int J Psychoanal 33:439, 1952
Larsen R: Ethical issues in psychiatry and occupational medicine. Occupational Medicine: State of the Art Reviews 3(4):719–726, 1988
Larson RC, Felton JS: Psychiatric Injury in the Workplace (State of the Art Reviews). Philadelphia, PA, Hanley & Belfus, October–December 1988
Lasky J: Guidelines for Handling Psychiatric Issues and Workers' Compensation Cases. Rancho Palos Verdes, CA, Lex-Com Enterprises, 1988
Levi L: Work, stress, and health. Scand J Work Environ Health 10(6, spec no), 1984
Levi J (ed): Stress and Distress in Response to Psychosocial Stimuli. New York, Pergamon, 1972
Levinson H: Men, Management, and Mental Health. Cambridge, MA, Harvard University Press, 1962
Levinson H: Organizational Diagnosis. Cambridge, MA, Harvard University Press, 1972
Longaker WD: The full time psychiatrist in industry. J Occup Med 14(3), March 1972
Maccoby M: Why Work? Motivating and Leading the New Generation. New York, Touchstone Books, Simon & Schuster, 1988
Manuso JS: Affirmative action and corporate emotional health programs. J Occup Med 22(10):653–656, 1980
Matteson MT, Ivancevich JM: Controlling Work Stress: Effective Human Resources and Management Strategies. San Francisco, CA, Jossey-Bass, 1988
Mayo E: The Human Problems of an Industrial Civilization. New York, Macmillan, 1934
McGregor D: Professional Manager. New York, McGraw-Hill, 1967
McLean AA: Occupational mental health: review of an emerging art, in Occupational Psychiatry. Edited by Collins RT. Boston, MA, Little, Brown, 1969
McLean AA: Occupational psychiatry, in Comprehensive Textbook of Psychiatry, Vol 3. Edited by Freedman A, Kaplan H, Saddock B. Baltimore, MD, Williams & Wilkins, pp 2368–2375, 1975
McLean AA: The psychiatrist's role in occupational mental health. New Dir Ment Health Serv 20:57–63, 1983

McLean AA: Report of the Task Force on Psychiatry and Industry, APA Council on National Affairs. Am J Psychiatry 141:1139–1144, 1984
McLean AA, Taylor GC: Mental Health in Industry. New York, McGraw-Hill, 1958
Menninger K: Work as a sublimation. Bull Menninger Clin 6:170–182, 1942
Menninger WC, Levinson H: Human Understanding in Industry: A Guide for Supervisors. Chicago, IL, Science Research Associates, 1957
Miller FH: The rights of the employee as patient. Occup Health Nurs 25(12):11–13, 1977
Morris LE: Industrial Stress Injuries. Los Gatos, CA, Bourne & Atherton, 1989
Murphy HB: The decline of industrial psychiatry. Psychol Med 3(4):405–410, 1973
National Clearinghouse for Mental Health Information: A selected bibliography on occupational mental health (Public Health Service Publ No 1338). Bethesda, MD, National Institute of Mental Health, 1965
Oberndorf C: The psychopathology of work. Bull Menninger Clin 15:77–89, 1951
O'Conner RB: The medical department and a psychiatric program. International Psychiatric Clinics 6(4):43–47, 1969
O'Donnell M, Ainsworth T: Health Promotion in the Work Place. New York, Wiley, 1984
Parmeggiani L: Current problems of the electronic treatment of data in occupational health. Med Lav 76(4):267–672, 1985
Ray JS: Having problems with worker performance? try an EAP. Administrative Management 43:17–49, 1982
Report of the Committee on Occupational Psychiatry: Employee Assistance Programs and the role of the psychiatrist. Am J Psychiatry 146(5):690–694, 1989
Roeske N: Two cultures. Psychiatric Annals 14(5), 1984
Roethlisberger FJ: The education of a clinician. Unpublished paper, Harvard Business School, 1970
Roethlisberger FJ, Dickson WJ: Management and the Worker. Cambridge, MA, Harvard University Press, 1939
Rohrlich JB: Work and Love: The Crucial Balance. New York, Summit Books, 1980
Roman PM: Ethics in worksite health programming: who is served? Health Educ Q 14(1):57–70, 1987
Ross WD: Practical Psychiatry for Industrial Physicians. Springfield, IL, Charles C Thomas, 1956
Schuler RS: Dealing with the effects of work-related stress. American Journal of Medical Technology 48(3):177–182, 1982

Seward JP: Occupational stress, in Occupational Medicine. Edited by LaDou J. Norwalk, CT, Appleton & Lange, 1990

Sherman M: A review of industrial psychiatry. Am J Psychiatry 83:701–710, 1927

Shestak AB: Psychiatry issues and organized labor. J Occup Med 21(1):48–51, 1979

Silverstein MA: Medical records and confidentiality [letter]. J Occup Med 26(11):790, 1984

Simon HA: The New Science of Management Decisions. New York, Harper & Row, 1960

Sloan SJ: Stress coping strategies in commercial airline pilots. J Occup Med 28(1):49–52, 1986

Smejda H: How one hospital sells its expertise to industry. Hospital Financial Management 31:8–12, 1977

Smith RS Jr: The psychiatrically impaired injured worker, part I: background and data review. W V Med J 75(6):154–158, 1979

Southard EE: The modern specialist in unrest: a place for the psychiatrist in industry. Mental Hygiene 4:550–563, 1920

Spector PE: Relation of job stressors to affective, health, and performance outcomes. J Appl Psychol 73(1):11–19, 1988

Spending to cut mental health costs: employer finds quality care the best buy. Wall Street Journal, December 13, 1989

Sprehe DJ: Workers' compensation: a psychiatric follow-up study. Int J Law Psychiatry 7(2):165–178, 1984

Stogdill RM: Personal factors associated with leadership. J Psychol 25:35–71, 1948

Tanay E: Psychiatric aspects of the role of industrial physicians. J Occup Med 14(3):207–211, 1972

Terkel S: Working. New York, Pantheon Books, 1972

The relationship between job loss and physical and mental illness. Hosp Community Psychiatry 34(5):438–441, 1983

Trist EL: Organizational Choice. London, Tavistock Publications, 1963

Tubbs AL: How physician and therapist team up in company setting. Occup Health Saf 48(3):63–67, 1979

Walton RE: Work innovations in the United States. Harvard Business Review, July–August 1979, p 88

Weiland GJ: Psychiatric consultation in the federal government. Occupational Mental Health 3(3):11–13, 1973

Weiner HJ, Akaba SH, Sommer JJ: Mental Health Care in the World of Work. New York, Association Press, 1973

Zaupta AJ: Job stress and task interest: two factors in work life quality. Am J Community Psychol 14(4):77–93, 1986

GAP Committees and Membership

Committee on Adolescence

Warren J. Gadpaille, Denver, CO, *Chairperson*
Ian A. Canino, New York, NY
Harvey Horowitz, Philadelphia, PA
Sarah Huertas-Goldman, San Juan, PR
Paulina F. Kernberg, New York, NY
Clarice J. Kestenbaum, New York, NY
Richard C. Marohn, Chicago, IL
Silvio J. Onesti, Jr., Belmont, MA

Committee on Aging

Gene D. Cohen, Washington, DC, *Chairperson*
Karen Blank, West Hartford, CT
Charles M. Gaitz, Houston, TX
Gary Gottlieb, Philadelphia, PA
Ira R. Katz, Philadelphia, PA
Andrew F. Leuchter, Los Angeles, CA
Gabe J. Maletta, Minneapolis, MN
Richard A. Margolin, Nashville, TN
Kenneth M. Sakauye, New Orleans, LA
Charles A. Shamoian, Larchmont, NY
F. Conyers Thompson, Jr., Atlanta, GA

Committee on Alcoholism and the Addictions

Joseph Westermeyer, Minneapolis, MN, *Chairperson*
Susan J. Blumenthal, Washington, DC
Richard J. Frances, Newark, NJ
Marc Galanter, New York, NY
Earl A. Loomis, Jr., Augusta, GA
Robert Millman, New York, NY
Edgar P. Nace, Dallas, TX

Peter Steinglass, Washington, DC
John S. Tamerin, Greenwich, CT

Committee on Child Psychiatry

Peter E. Tanguay, Los Angeles, CA, *Chairperson*
James M. Bell, Canaan, NY
Mark Blotcky, Dallas, TX
Harlow Donald Dunton, New York, NY
Joseph Fischhoff, Detroit, MI
Joseph M. Green, Madison, WI
John F. McDermott, Jr., Honolulu, HI
David A. Mrazek, Denver, CO
Cynthia R. Pfeffer, White Plains, NY
John Schowalter, New Haven, CT
Theodore Shapiro, New York, NY
Leonore Terr, San Francisco, CA

Committee on College Students

Earle Silber, Chevy Chase, MD, *Chairperson*
Robert L. Arnstein, Hamden, CT
Varda Backus, La Jolla, CA
Harrison P. Eddy, New York, NY
Myron B. Liptzin, Chapel Hill, NC
Malkah Tolpin Notman, Brookline, MA
Gloria C. Onque, Pittsburgh, PA
Elizabeth Aub Reid, Cambridge, MA
Lorraine D. Siggins, New Haven, CT
Tom G. Stauffer, White Plains, NY

Committee on Cultural Psychiatry

Ezra Griffith, New Haven, CT, *Chairperson*
Edward Foulks, New Orleans, LA
Roberto Jimenez, San Antonio, TX
Pedro Ruiz, Houston, TX
Ronald Wintrob, Providence, RI
Joe Yamamoto, Los Angeles, CA

Committee on the Family

Herta A. Guttman, Montreal, PQ, *Chairperson*
W. Robert Beavers, Dallas, TX

Ellen M. Berman, Merion, PA
Frederick Gottlieb, Los Angeles, CA
Henry U. Grunebaum, Cambridge, MA
Judith Landau-Stanton, Rochester, NY
Ann L. Price, Avon, CT
Lyman C. Wynne, Rochester, NY

Committee on Government Policy

Roger Peele, Washington, DC, *Chairperson*
Thomas L. Clannon, San Francisco, CA
Naomi Heller, Washington, DC
John P. D. Shemo, Charlottesville, VA
William W. Van Stone, Washington, DC

Committee on Handicaps

Meyer S. Gunther, Wilmette, IL, *Chairperson*
Bryan King, Los Angeles, CA
Robert Nesheim, Duluth, MN
William H. Sack, Portland, OR
William A. Sonis, Philadelphia, PA
Margaret L. Stuber, Los Angeles, CA
Thomas G. Webster, Washington, DC
Henry H. Work, Bethesda, MD

Committee on Human Sexuality

Bertram H. Schaffner, New York, NY, *Chairperson*
Paul L. Adams, Galveston, TX
Debra Carter, Farmington, NM
Richard Friedman, New York, NY
Peggy Hanley-Hackenbruck, Portland, OR
Joan A. Lang, Galveston, TX
Stuart E. Nichols, New York, NY
Harris B. Peck, New Rochelle, NY
Terry S. Stein, East Lansing, MI

Committee on International Relations

Vamik D. Volkan, Charlottesville, VA, *Chairperson*
Salman Akhtar, Philadelphia, PA
Robert M. Dorn, El Macero, CA

John S. Kafka, Washington, DC
Otto F. Kernberg, White Plains, NY
Roy W. Menninger, Topeka, KS
Peter A. Olsson, Houston, TX
Rita R. Rogers, Palos Verdes Estates, CA
Stephen B. Shanfield, San Antonio, TX

Committee on Medical Education

Steven L. Dubovsky, Denver, CO, *Chairperson*
Leah Dickstein, Louisville, KY
Saul I. Harrison, Torrance, CA
David R. Hawkins, Chicago, IL
Harold I. Lief, Philadelphia, PA
Carol C. Nadelson, Boston, MA
Carolyn B. Robinowitz, Washington, DC
Stephen C. Scheiber, Deerfield, IL
Sidney L. Werkman, Washington, DC

Committee on Mental Health Services

W. Walter Menninger, Topeka, KS, *Chairperson*
Mary Jane England, Roseland, NJ
Robert O. Friedel, Richmond, VA
John M. Hamilton, Columbia, MD
Jose Maria Santiago, Tucson, AZ
Steven S. Sharfstein, Baltimore, MD
George F. Wilson, Somerville, NJ
Jack A. Wolford, Pittsburgh, PA

Committee on Occupational Psychiatry

Barrie S. Greiff, M.D., Newton, MA, *Chairperson*
Peter L. Brill, M.D., Radnor, PA
Duane Q. Hagen, M.D., St. Louis, MO
R. Edward Huffman, M.D., Asheville, NC
Robert Larsen, M.D., San Francisco, CA
David E. Morrison, M.D., Palatine, IL
David B. Robbins, M.D., Chappaqua, NY
Jay B. Rohrlich, M.D., New York, NY
Clarence J. Rowe, M.D., St. Paul, MN
Jeffrey L. Speller, M.D., Cambridge, MA

Committee on Planning and Communications

Robert W. Gibson, Towson, MD, *Chairperson*
C. Knight Aldrich, Charlottesville, VA
Allan Beigel, Tucson, AZ
Doyle I. Carson, Dallas, TX
Paul J. Fink, Philadelphia, PA
Robert S. Garber, Longboat Key, FL
Richard K. Goodstein, Belle Mead, NJ
Harvey L. Ruben, New Haven, CT
Melvin Sabshin, Washington, DC
Michael R. Zales, Quechee, VT

Committee on Preventive Psychiatry

Naomi Rae-Grant, London, ON, *Chairperson*
Viola W. Bernard, New York, NY
Stephen Fleck, New Haven, CT
Brian J. McConville, Cincinnati, OH
David R. Offord, Hamilton, ON
Morton M. Silverman, Chicago, IL
Warren T. Vaughan, Jr., Portola Valley, CA

Committee on Psychiatry and the Community

David G. Greenfield, Guilford, CT, *Chairperson*
Stephen Goldfinger, Boston, MA
H. Richard Lamb, Los Angeles, CA
Kenneth Minkoff, Woburn, MA
John C. Nemiah, Hanover, NH
John J. Schwab, Louisville, KY
John A. Talbott, Baltimore, MD
Allan Tasman, Louisville, KY

Committee on Psychiatry and the Law

Joseph Satten, San Francisco, CA, *Chairperson*
J. Richard Ciccone, Rochester, NY
Carl P. Malmquist, Minneapolis, MN
Jeffrey Metzner, Denver, CO
Herbert C. Modlin, Topeka, KS
Jonas R. Rappeport, Baltimore, MD
Phillip J. Resnick, Cleveland, OH

Robert I. Simon, Bethesda, MD
William D. Weitzel, Lexington, KY

Committee on Psychiatry and Religion

Richard C. Lewis, New Haven, CT, *Chairperson*
Naleen N. Andrade, Honolulu, HI
Keith G. Meador, Nashville, TN
Abigail R. Ostow, Belmont, MA
Sally K. Severino, White Plains, NY
Clyde R. Snyder, Fayetteville, NC
Herzl Spiro, Milwaukee, WI
Edwin R. Wallace IV, Augusta, GA

Committee on Psychopathology

Robert A. Dorwart, Cambridge, MA, *Chairperson*
David A. Adler, Boston, MA
Jeffrey Berlant, Boise, ID
John P. Docherty, Nashua, NH
James M. Ellison, Watertown, MA
Howard H. Goldman, Potomac, MD
Samuel G. Siris, Glen Oaks, NY

Committee on Public Education

Steven E. Katz, New York, NY, *Chairperson*
David Baron, Ambler, PA
Jack W. Bonner III, Asheville, NC
Jeffrey L. Geller, Worcester, MA
Jeanne Leventhal, Hayward, CA
Elise K. Richman, Scarsdale, NY
Boris G. Rifkin, Branford, CT
Andrew E. Slaby, Summit, NJ
Robert A. Solow, Los Angeles, CA
Calvin R. Sumner, Buckhannon, WV

Committee on Research

Zebulon Taintor, New York, NY, *Chairperson*
Robert Cancro, New York, NY
John H. Greist, Madison, WI
Jerry M. Lewis, Dallas, TX
John G. Looney, Durham, NC

Committee on Social Issues

Martha J. Kirkpatrick, Los Angeles, CA, *Chairperson*
Ian E. Alger, New York, NY
William R. Beardslee, Waban, MA
Roderic Gorney, Los Angeles, CA
H. James Lurie, Seattle, WA
Ted Nadelson, Boston, MA
Perry Ottenberg, Philadelphia, PA
Kendon W. Smith, Pearl River, NY

Committee on Therapeutic Care

William W. Richards, Anchorage, AK, *Chairperson*
Bernard Bandler, Cambridge, MA
Thomas E. Curtis, Chapel Hill, NC
Donald C. Fidler, Morgantown, WV
Alan Gruenberg, Philadelphia, PA
Donald W. Hammersley, Washington, DC
William B. Hunter III, Albuquerque, NM
Roberto L. Jimenez, San Antonio, TX
Milton Kramer, Cincinnati, OH
John Lipkin, Perry Point, MA

Committee on Therapy

Jules R. Bemporad, White Plains, NY, *Chairperson*
Gerald Adler, Boston, MA
Eugene B. Feigelson, Brooklyn, NY
Robert Michels, New York, NY
Andrew P. Morrison, Cambridge, MA
William C. Offenkrantz, Scottsdale, AZ
Allan D. Rosenblatt, La Jolla, CA

GINSBURG FELLOWS

Charlissa Allen, Columbia, MO *(Committee on College Students)*
Linda Brzustowicz, New York, NY *(Committee on Public Education)*
David L. Carlson, Fargo, ND *(Committee on Alcoholism and the Addictions)*
Josepha A. Cheong, Gainesville, FL *(Committee on Aging)*

Henry Chung, White Plains, NY *(Committee on Cultural Psychiatry)*
Craig L. Donnelly, Durham, NC *(Committee on Child Psychiatry)*
Benjamin Druss, New Haven, CT *(Committee on Occupational Psychiatry)*
Jeffrey Dutton, Seattle, WA *(Committee on Government Policy)*
Mark A. Frye, Los Angeles, CA *(Committee on Medical Education)*
Sanjay Gulati, Cambridge, MA *(Committee on Handicaps)*
Scott T. Hedges, Louisville, KY *(Committee on International Relations)*
Anthony G. Hempel, Galveston, TX *(Committee on Psychiatry and the Law)*
Mary J. Kajawa, Cleveland, OH *(Committee on Social Issues)*
Aryeh L. Levenson, Baltimore, MD *(Committee on Psychiatry and Religion)*
George K. Makini, Honolulu, HI *(Committee on Preventive Psychiatry)*
Anu Ahluwalia Mator, Houston, TX *(Committee on Psychiatry and the Community)*
Tanya K. Murphy, Gainesville, FL *(Committee on Committee on the Family)*
Paul E. Quinlan, Ann Arbor, MI *(Committee on Therapy)*
Justin Richardson, Cambridge, MA *(Committee on Human Sexuality)*
Andrew Rosenzweig, Pittsburgh, PA *(Committee on Therapeutic Care)*
Melissa D. Rowland, Charleston, SC *(Committee on Mental Health Services)*
Marc S. Sageman, Philadelphia, PA *(Committee on Psychopathology)*
Martha Schinagle, Boston, MA *(Committee on Adolescence)*
Steven Simpson, Calgary, AB *(Committee on Research)*
George Thompson, Topeka, KS *(Committee on Planning and Communications)*

Contributing Members

Gene Abroms, Ardmore, PA
Carlos C. Alden, Jr., Buffalo, NY
Kenneth Z. Altshuler, Dallas, TX
Francis F. Barnes, Washington, DC
Spencer Bayles, Houston, TX
C. Christian Beels, New York, NY

Elissa P. Benedek, Ann Arbor, MI
Renee L. Binder, San Francisco, CA
H. Keith H. Brodie, Durham, NC
Charles M. Bryant, San Francisco, CA
Ewald W. Busse, Durham, NC
Robert N. Butler, New York, NY
Eugene M. Caffey, Jr., Bowie, MD
Robert J. Campbell, New York, NY
James P. Cattell, San Diego, CA
Ian L. W. Clancey, Maitland, ON
Sanford I. Cohen, Coral Gables, FL
Lee Combrinck-Graham, Evanston, IL
Charles M. Culver, Hanover, NH
Robert E. Drake, Hanover, NH
James S. Eaton, Jr., Washington, DC
Lloyd C. Elam, Nashville, TN
Joseph T. English, New York, NY
Sherman C. Feinstein, Highland Park, IL
Archie R. Foley, New York, NY
Sidney Furst, Bronx, NY
Henry J. Gault, Highland Park, IL
Ira D. Glick, New York, NY
Judith H. Gold, Halifax, NS
Alexander Gralnick, Port Chester, NY
Milton Greenblatt, Sylmar, CA
Lawrence F. Greenleigh, Los Angeles, CA
Stanley I. Greenspan, Bethesda, MD
Jon E. Gudeman, Milwaukee, WI
William Hetznecker, Merion Station, PA
Johanna A. Hoffman, Scottsdale, AZ
Keith Johansen, Dallas, TX
Edward J. Khantzian, Haverhill, MA
James A. Knight, New Orleans, LA
Othilda M. Krug, Cincinnati, OH
Anthony F. Lehman, Baltimore, MD
Alan I. Levenson, Tucson, AZ
Norman L. Loux, Sellersville, PA
Albert J. Lubin, Woodside, CA
John Mack, Chestnut Hill, MA
John A. MacLeod, Cincinnati, OH
Charles A. Malone, Barrington, RI
Peter A. Martin, Lake Orion, MI
Alan A. McLean, Gig Harbor, WA

David Mendell, Houston, TX
Mary E. Mercer, Nyack, NY
Derek Miller, Chicago, IL
Steven M. Mirin, Belmont, MA
Richard D. Morrill, Boston, MA
Robert J. Nathan, Philadelphia, PA
Joseph D. Noshpitz, Washington, DC
Mortimer Ostow, Bronx, NY
Bernard L. Pacella, New York, NY
Kathleen A. Pajer, Pittsburgh, PA
Herbert Pardes, New York, NY
Norman L. Paul, Lexington, MA
Marvin E. Perkins, Salem, VA
George H. Pollock, Chicago, IL
Becky Potter, Tucson, AZ
David N. Ratnavale, Bethesda, MD
W. Donald Ross, Cincinnati, OH
Loren Roth, Pittsburgh, PA
Charles Shagass, Philadelphia, PA
Albert J. Silverman, Ann Arbor, MI
Benson R. Snyder, Cambridge, MA
David A. Soskis, Bala Cynwyd, PA
Jeffrey L. Speller, Cambridge, MA
Jeanne Spurlock, Washington, DC
Brandt F. Steele, Denver, CO
Alan A. Stone, Cambridge, MA
Perry C. Talkington, Dallas, TX
John A. Talbott, Baltimore, MD
Bryce Templeton, Philadelphia, PA
Prescott W. Thompson, Portland, OR
John A. Turner, San Francisco, CA
Kenneth N. Vogtsberger, San Antonio, TX
Andrew S. Watson, Ann Arbor, MI
Paul Tyler Wilson, Bethesda, MD
Ann Marie Wolf-Schatz, Conshohocken, PA
Sherwyn M. Woods, Los Angeles, CA
Kent A. Zimmerman, Menlo Park, CA
Howard Zonana, New Haven, CT

Life Members

C. Knight Aldrich, Charlottesville, VA
Robert L. Arnstein, Hamden, CT

Bernard Bandler, Cambridge, MA
Walter E. Barton, Hartland, VT
Viola W. Bernard, New York, NY
Henry W. Brosin, Tucson, AZ
John Donnelly, Hartford, CT
Merrill T. Eaton, Omaha, NE
O. Spurgeon English, Narberth, PA
Stephen Fleck, New Haven, CT
Jerome Frank, Baltimore, MD
Robert S. Garber, Longboat Key, FL
Robert I. Gibson, Towson, MD
Margaret M. Lawrence, Pomona, NY
Jerry M. Lewis, Dallas, TX
Harold I. Lief, Philadelphia, PA
Judd Marmor, Los Angeles, CA
Herbert C. Modlin, Topeka, KS
John C. Nemiah, Hanover, NH
William C. Offenkrantz, Scottsdale, AZ
Mabel Ross, Sun City, AZ
Julius Schreiber, Washington, DC
Robert E. Switzer, Dunn Loring, VA
Jack A. Wolford, Pittsburgh, PA
Henry H. Work, Bethesda, MD

BOARD OF DIRECTORS

Officers

President
John Schowalter
P.O. Box 3333
Yale Child Study Center
New Haven, CT 06510

President-Elect
Doyle I. Carson
Timberlawn Psychiatric Hospital
Box 151489
Dallas, TX 75315-1489

Secretary
Stephen C. Scheiber
ABPN
500 Lake Cook Road
Deerfield, IL 60015

Treasurer
Jack W. Bonner III
The Oaks Treatment Center
1407 West Stassney Lane
Austin, TX 78745

Board Members
Ian Alger
Naomi Rae-Grant
José Santiago
Joe Yamamoto

Past Presidents
*William C. Menninger 1946–51
Jack R. Ewalt 1951–53
Walter E. Barton 1953–55
*Sol W. Ginsburg 1955–57
*Dana L. Farnsworth 1957–59
*Marion E. Kenworthy 1959–61
Henry W. Brosin 1961–63
*Leo H. Bartemeier 1963–65
Robert S. Garber 1965–67
Herbert C. Modlin 1967–69
John Donnelly 1969–71
George Tarjan 1971–73
Judd Marmor 1973–75
John C. Nemiah 1975–77
Jack A. Wolford 1977–79
Robert W. Gibson 1979–81

* Deceased.

*Jack Weinberg 1981–82
Henry H. Work 1982–85
Michael R. Zales 1985–87
Jerry M. Lewis 1987–89
Carolyn B. Robinowitz 1989–91
Allan Beigel 1991–93

PUBLICATIONS BOARD

Chairperson
C. Knight Aldrich
Health Sciences Center
Box 414
Charlottesville, VA 22908

Robert L. Arnstein
Mark Blotcky
Ezra Griffith
Steve Katz
W. Walter Menninger

Consultants
John C. Nemiah
Henry H. Work

Ex-Officio
Allan Beigel
Carolyn B. Robinowitz

CONTRIBUTORS

Abbott Laboratories
American Charitable Fund
Dr. and Mrs. Richard Aron
Mr. Robert C. Baker

* Deceased.

Bristol-Myers Squibb Co.
Maurice Falk Medical Fund
Mrs. Carol Gold
Edith F. Goldensohn
Grove Foundation, Inc.
Miss Gayle Groves
Ittleson Foundation, Inc.
Mr. Barry Jacobson
Mrs. Allan H. Kalmus
Marion E. Kenworthy–Sarah H. Swift Foundation, Inc.
Mr. Larry Korman
McNeil Pharmaceutical
Murel Foundation
Phillips Foundation
Sandoz Corporation
Smith Kline Beckman Corporation
Tappanz Foundation, Inc.
The Upjohn Company
van Ameringen Foundation, Inc.
Wyeth-Ayerst Laboratories
Mr. and Mrs. William A. Zales

GAP Publications

Introduction to Occupational Psychiatry (GAP Report 138, 1994), Formulated by the Committee on Psychiatry in Industry

Forced Into Treatment: The Role of Coercion in Clinical Practice (GAP Report 137, 1994), Formulated by the Committee on Governmental Policy

Resident's Guide to Treatment of People With Chronic Mental Illness (GAP Report 136, 1993), Formulated by the Committee on Psychiatry and the Community

Caring for People With Physical Impairment: The Journey Back (GAP Report 135, 1992), Formulated by the Committee on Handicaps

Beyond Symptom Suppression: Improving Long-Term Outcomes of Schizophrenia (GAP Report 134, 1992), Formulated by the Committee on Psychopathology

Psychotherapy in the Future (GAP Report 133, 1992), Formulated by the Committee on Therapy

Leaders and Followers: A Psychiatric Perspective on Religious Cults (GAP Report 132, 1992), Formulated by the Committee on Psychiatry and Religion

The Mental Health Professional and the Legal System (GAP Report 131, 1991), Formulated by the Committee on Psychiatry and the Law

***Psychotherapy With College Students** (GAP Report 130, 1990), Formulated by the Committee on the College Student

A Casebook in Psychiatric Ethics (GAP Report 129, 1990), Formulated by the Committee on Medical Education

***Suicide and Ethnicity in the United States** (GAP Report 128, 1989), Formulated by the Committee on Cultural Psychiatry

Psychiatric Prevention and the Family Life Cycle: Risk Reduction by Frontline Practitioners (GAP Report 127, 1989), Formulated by the Committee on Preventive Psychiatry

---

*Title is out of print.

†Available from Books on Demand, University Microfilms International, 300 North Zeeb Road, Ann Arbor, MI 48106-1346 (800-521-0600, ext. 3492).

Psychiatric Prevention and the Family Life Cycle: Risk Reduction by Frontline Practitioners (GAP Report 127, 1989), Formulated by the Committee on Preventive Psychiatry

How Old Is Old Enough? The Ages of Rights and Responsibilities (GAP Report 126, 1989), Formulated by the Committee on Child Psychiatry

The Psychiatric Treatment of Alzheimer's Disease (GAP Report 125, 1988), Formulated by the Committee on Aging

Speaking Out for Psychiatry: A Handbook for Involvement With the Mass Media (GAP Report 124, 1987), Formulated by the Committee on Public Education

Us and Them: The Psychology of Ethnonationalism (GAP Report 123, 1987), Formulated by the Committee on International Relations

Psychiatry and Mental Health Professionals (GAP Report 122, 1987), Formulated by the Committee on Governmental Agencies

Interactive Fit: A Guide to Nonpsychotic Chronic Patients (GAP Report 121, 1987), Formulated by the Committee on Psychopathology

Teaching Psychotherapy in Contemporary Psychiatric Residency Training (GAP Report 120, 1986), Formulated by the Committee on Therapy

A Family Affair: Helping Families Cope With Mental Illness: A Guide for the Professions (GAP Report 119, 1986), Formulated by the Committee on Psychiatry and the Community

Crises of Adolescence—Teenage Pregnancy: Impact on Adolescent Development (GAP Report 118, 1986), Formulated by the Committee on Adolescence

The Family, the Patient, and the Psychiatric Hospital: Toward a New Model (GAP Report 117, 1985), Formulated by the Committee on Family

*†**Research and the Complex Causality of the Schizophrenias** (GAP Report 116, 1984), Formulated by the Committee on Research

***Friends and Lovers in the College Years** (GAP Report 115, 1983), Formulated by the Committee on the College Student

***Mental Health and Aging: Approaches to Curriculum Development** (GAP Report 114, 1983), Formulated by the Committee on Aging

Community Psychiatry: A Reappraisal (GAP Report 113, 1983), Formulated by the Committee on Psychiatry and the Community

The Child and Television Drama (GAP Report 112, 1982), Formulated by the Committee on Social Issues

***The Process of Child Therapy** (GAP Report 111, 1982), Formulated by the Committee on Child Psychiatry

The Positive Aspects of Long Term Hospitalization in the Public Sector for Chronic Psychiatric Patients (GAP Report 110, 1982), Formulated by the Committee on Psychopathology

Job Loss—A Psychiatric Perspective (GAP Report 109, 1982), Formulated by the Committee on Psychiatry in Industry

A Survival Manual for Medical Students (GAP Report 108, 1982), Formulated by the Committee on Medical Education

INTERFACES: A Communication Casebook for Mental Health Decision Makers (GAP Report 107, 1981), Formulated by the Committee on Mental Health Services

[*]**Divorce, Child Custody and the Family** (GAP Report 106, 1980), Formulated by the Committee on Family

[*]**Mental Health and Primary Medical Care** (GAP Report 105, 1980), Formulated by the Committee on Preventive Psychiatry

Psychiatric Consultation in Mental Retardation (GAP Report 104, 1979), Formulated by the Committee on Mental Retardation

[*]**Self-Involvement in the Middle East Conflict** (GAP Report 103, 1978), Formulated by the Committee on International Relations

The Chronic Mental Patient in the Community (GAP Report 102, 1978), Formulated by the Committee on Psychiatry and the Community

Power and Authority in Adolescence: The Origins and Resolutions of Intergenerational Conflict (GAP Report 101, 1978), Formulated by the Committee on Adolescence

[*]**Psychotherapy and Its Financial Feasibility Within the National Health Care System** (GAP Report 100, 1978), Formulated by the Committee on Therapy

[*†]**What Price Compensation?** (GAP Report 99, 1977), Formulated by the Committee on Psychiatry in Industry

[*]**Psychiatry and Sex Psychopath Legislation: The 30s to the 80s** (GAP Report 98, 1977), Formulated by the Committee on Psychiatry and Law

Mysticism: Spiritual Quest or Psychic Disorder? (GAP Report 97, 1976), Formulated by the Committee on Psychiatry and Religion

[*†]**Recertification: A Look at the Issues** (GAP Report 96, 1976), Formulated by the Ad hoc Committee on Recertification

[*†]**The Effect of the Method of Payment on Mental Health Care Practice** (GAP Report 95, 1975), Formulated by the Committee on Governmental Agencies

[*]**The Psychiatrist and Public Welfare Agencies** (GAP Report 94, 1975), Formulated by the Committee on Psychiatry and the Community

[*]**Pharmacotherapy and Psychotherapy: Paradoxes, Problems and Progress** (GAP Report 93, 1975), Formulated by the Committee on Research

*__The Educated Woman: Prospects and Problems__ (GAP Report 92, 1975), Formulated by the Committee on the College Student

*†__The Community Worker: A Response to Human Need__ (GAP Report 91, 1974), Formulated by the Committee on Therapeutic Care

*†__Problems of Psychiatric Leadership__ (GAP Report 90, 1974), Formulated by the Committee on Therapy

*__Misuse of Psychiatry in the Criminal Courts: Competency to Stand Trial__ (GAP Report 89, 1974), Formulated by the Committee on Psychiatry and Law

Assessment of Sexual Function: A Guide to Interviewing (GAP Report 88, 1973), Formulated by the Committee on Medical Education

From Diagnosis to Treatment: An Approach to Treatment Planning for the Emotionally Disturbed Child (GAP Report 87, 1973), Formulated by the Committee on Child Psychiatry

*†__Humane Reproduction__ (GAP Report 86, 1973), Formulated by the Committee on Preventive Psychiatry

*__The Welfare System and Mental Health__ (GAP Report 85, 1973), Formulated by the Committee on Psychiatry and Social Work

*†__The Joys and Sorrows of Parenthood__ (GAP Report 84, 1973), Formulated by the Committee on Public Education

*__The VIP With Psychiatric Impairment__ (GAP Report 83, 1973), Formulated by the Committee on Governmental Agencies

*__Crisis in Child Mental Health: A Critical Assessment__ (GAP Report 82, 1972), Formulated by the Ad hoc Committee

The Aged and Community Mental Health: A Guide to Program Development (GAP Report 81, 1971), Formulated by the Committee on Aging

*__Drug Misuse: A Psychiatric View of a Modern Dilemma__ (GAP Report 80, 1970), Formulated by the Committee on Mental Health Services

*†__Toward a Public Policy on Mental Health Care of the Elderly__ (GAP Report 79, 1970), Formulated by the Committee on Aging

The Field of Family Therapy (GAP Report 78, 1970), Formulated by the Committee on Family

*__Toward Therapeutic Care__ (2nd Edition—No. 51 revised) (GAP Report 77, 1970), Formulated by the Committee on Therapeutic Care

*__The Case History Method in the Study of Family Process__ (GAP Report 76, 1970), Formulated by the Committee on Family

*__The Right to Abortion: A Psychiatric View__ (GAP Report 75, 1969), Formulated by the Committee on Psychiatry and Law

*†__The Psychiatrist and Public Issues__ (GAP Report 74, 1969), Formulated by the Committee on International Relations

*†**Psychotherapy and the Dual Research Tradition** (GAP Report 73, 1969), Formulated by the Committee on Therapy

***Crisis in Psychiatric Hospitalization** (GAP Report 72, 1969), Formulated by the Committee on Therapeutic Care

***On Psychotherapy and Casework** (GAP Report 71, 1969), Formulated by the Committee on Psychiatry and Social Work

***The Nonpsychotic Alcoholic Patient and the Mental Hospital** (GAP Report 70, 1968), Formulated by the Committee on Mental Health Services

***The Dimensions of Community Psychiatry** (GAP Report 69, 1968), Formulated by the Committee on Preventive Psychiatry

***Normal Adolescence** (GAP Report 68, 1968), Formulated by the Committee on Adolescence

The Psychic Function of Religion in Mental Illness and Health (GAP Report 67, 1968), Formulated by the Committee on Psychiatry and Religion

***Mild Mental Retardation: A Growing Challenge to the Physician** (GAP Report 66, 1967), Formulated by the Committee on Mental Retardation

*†**The Recruitment and Training of the Research Psychiatrist** (GAP Report 65, 1967), Formulated by the Committee on Psychopathology

***Education for Community Psychiatry** (GAP Report 64, 1967), Formulated by the Committee on Medical Education

*†**Psychiatric Research and the Assessment of Change** (GAP Report 63, 1966), Formulated by the Committee on Research

***Psychopathological Disorders in Childhood: Theoretical Considerations and a Proposed Classification** (GAP Report 62, 1966), Formulated by the Committee on Child Psychiatry

***Laws Governing Hospitalization of the Mentally Ill** (GAP Report 61, 1966), Formulated by the Committee on Psychiatry and Law

***Sex and the College Student** (GAP Report 60, 1965), Formulated by the Committee on the College Student

*†**Psychiatry and the Aged: An Introductory Approach** (GAP Report 59, 1965), Formulated by the Committee on Aging

*†**Medical Practice and Psychiatry: The Impact of Changing Demands** (GAP Report 58, 1964), Formulated by the Committee on Public Education

Psychiatric Aspects of the Prevention of Nuclear War (GAP Report 57, 1964), Formulated by the Committee on Social Issues

***Mental Retardation: A Family Crisis—The Therapeutic Role of the Physician** (GAP Report 56, 1963), Formulated by the Committee on Mental Retardation

*Public Relations: A Responsibility of the Mental Hospital Administrator** (GAP Report 55, 1963), Formulated by the Committee on Hospitals

***The Preclinical Teaching of Psychiatry** (GAP Report 54, 1962), Formulated by the Committee on Medical Education

***Psychiatrists as Teachers in Schools of Social Work** (GAP Report 53, 1962), Formulated by the Committee on Psychiatry and Social Work

The College Experience: A Focus for Psychiatric Research (GAP Report 52, 1962), Formulated by the Committee on the College Student

***Toward Therapeutic Care: A Guide for Those Who Work With the Mentally Ill** (GAP Report 51, 1961), Formulated by the Committee on Therapeutic Care

***Problems of Estimating Changes in Frequency of Mental Disorders** (GAP Report 50, 1961), Formulated by the Committee on Preventive Psychiatry

***Reports in Psychotherapy: Initial Interviews** (GAP Report 49, 1961), Formulated by the Committee on Therapy

***Psychiatry and Religion: Some Steps Toward Mutual Understanding and Usefulness** (GAP Report 48, 1960), Formulated by the Committee on Psychiatry and Religion

***Preventive Psychiatry in the Armed Forces: With Some Implications for Civilian Use** (GAP Report 47, 1960), Formulated by the Committee on Governmental Agencies

***Administration of the Public Psychiatric Hospital** (GAP Report 46, 1960), Formulated by the Committee on Hospitals

***Confidentiality and Privileged Communication in the Practice of Psychiatry** (GAP Report 45, 1960), Formulated by the Committee on Psychiatry and Law

***The Psychiatrist and His Roles in a Mental Health Association** (GAP Report 44, 1960), Formulated by the Committee on Public Education

***Basic Considerations in Mental Retardation: A Preliminary Report** (GAP Report 43, 1959), Formulated by the Committee on Mental Retardation

***Some Observations on Controls in Psychiatric Research** (GAP Report 42, 1959), Formulated by the Committee on Research

***Working Abroad: A Discussion of Psychological Attitudes and Adaptation in New Situations** (GAP Report 41, 1958), Formulated by the Committee on International Relations

***Small Group Teaching in Psychiatry for Medical Students** (GAP Report 40, 1958), Formulated by the Committee on Medical Education

***The Psychiatrist's Interest in Leisure-Time Activities** (GAP Report 39, 1958), Formulated by the Committee on Public Education

The Diagnostic Process in Child Psychiatry (GAP Report 38, 1958), Formulated by the Committee on Child Psychiatry

*__Emotional Aspects of School Desegregation__ (an abbreviated and less technical version of Report No. 37) (GAP Report 37A, 1960), Formulated by the Committee on Social Issues

*__Psychiatric Aspects of School Desegregation__ (GAP Report 37, 1957), Formulated by the Committee on Social Issues

*__The Person With Epilepsy at Work__ (GAP Report 36, 1957), Formulated by the Committee on Psychiatry in Industry

*__The Psychiatrist in Mental Health Education: Suggestions on Collaboration With Teachers__ (GAP Report 35, 1956), Formulated by the Committee on Public Education

*__The Consultant Psychiatrist in a Family Service Agency__ (GAP Report 34, 1956), Formulated by the Committee on Psychiatry and Social Work

*__Therapeutic Use of the Self (A Concept for Teaching Patient Care)__ (GAP Report 33, 1955), Formulated by the Committee on Psychiatric Nursing

*__Considerations on Personality Development in College Students__ (GAP Report 32, 1955), Formulated by the Committee on the College Student

*__Trends and Issues in Psychiatric Residency Programs__ (GAP Report 31, 1955), Formulated by the Committee on Medical Education

*__Report on Homosexuality With Particular Emphasis on This Problem in Governmental Agencies__ (GAP Report 30, 1955), Formulated by the Committee on Governmental Agencies

*__The Psychiatrist in Mental Health Education__ (GAP Report 29, 1954), Formulated by the Committee on Public Education

*__The Use of Psychiatrists in Government in Relation to International Problems__ (GAP Report 28, 1954), Formulated by the Committee on International Relations

*__Integration and Conflict in Family Behavior__ (Reissued in 1968 as No. 27A) (GAP Report 27, 1954), Formulated by the Committee on Family

*__Criminal Responsibility and Psychiatric Expert Testimony__ (GAP Report 26, 1954), Formulated by the Committee on Psychiatry and Law

*__Collaborative Research in Psychopathology__ (GAP Report 25, 1954), Formulated by the Committee on Psychopathology

*__Control and Treatment of Tuberculosis in Mental Hospitals__ (GAP Report 24, 1954), Formulated by the Committee on Hospitals

*__Outline to Be Used as a Guide to the Evaluation of Treatment in a Public Psychiatric Hospital__ (GAP Report 23, 1953), Formulated by the Committee on Hospitals

*The Psychiatric Nurse in the Mental Hospital** (GAP Report 22, 1952), Formulated by the Committee on Psychiatric Nursing—Committee on Hospitals

***The Contribution of Child Psychiatry to Pediatric Training and Practice** (GAP Report 21, 1952), Formulated by the Committee on Child Psychiatry

***The Application of Psychiatry to Industry** (GAP Report 20, 1951), Formulated by the Committee on Psychiatry in Industry

***Introduction to the Psychiatric Aspects of Civil Defense** (GAP Report 19, 1951), Formulated by the Committee on Governmental Agencies

***Promotion of Mental Health in the Primary and Secondary Schools: An Evaluation of Four Projects** (GAP Report 18, 1951), Formulated by the Committee on Preventive Psychiatry

***The Role of Psychiatrists in Colleges and Universities** (GAP Report 17, 1951), Formulated by the Committee on Academic Education

***Psychiatric Social Work in the Psychiatric Clinic** (GAP Report 16, 1950), Formulated by the Committee on Psychiatry and Social Work

***Revised Electro-Shock Therapy Report** (GAP Report 15, 1950), Formulated by the Committee on Therapy

***The Problem of the Aged Patient in the Public Psychiatric Hospital** (GAP Report 14, 1950), Formulated by the Committee on Hospitals

***The Social Responsibility of Psychiatry: A Statement of Orientation** (GAP Report 13, 1950), Formulated by the Committee on Social Issues

***Basic Concepts in Child Psychiatry** (GAP Report 12, 1950), Formulated by the Committee on Child Psychiatry

***The Position of Psychiatrists in the Field of International Relations** (GAP Report 11, 1950), Formulated by the Committee on International Relations

***Psychiatrically Deviated Sex Offenders** (GAP Report 10, 1950), Formulated by the Committee on Forensic Psychiatry

***The Relation of Clinical Psychology to Psychiatry** (GAP Report 9, 1949), Formulated by the Committee on Clinical Psychology

***An Outline for Evaluation of a Community Program in Mental Hygiene** (GAP Report 8, 1949), Formulated by the Committee on Cooperation With Lay Groups

***Statistics Pertinent to Psychiatry in the United States** (GAP Report 7, 1949), Formulated by the Committee on Hospitals

***Research on Prefrontal Lobotomy** (GAP Report 6, 1948), Formulated by the Committee on Research

***Public Psychiatric Hospitals** (GAP Report 5, 1948), Formulated by the Committee on Hospitals

*__Commitment Procedures__ (GAP Report 4, 1948), Formulated by the Committee on Forensic Psychiatry
*__Report on Medical Education__ (GAP Report 3, 1948), Formulated by the Committee on Medical Education
*__The Psychiatric Social Worker in the Psychiatric Hospital__ (GAP Report 2, 1948), Formulated by the Committee on Psychiatric Social Work
*__Shock Therapy__ (GAP Report 1, 1947), Formulated by the Committee on Therapy
Index to GAP Publications #1–80

Symposia Reports

The Right to Die: Decision and Decision Makers (S-12, 1973), Formulated by the Committee on Aging
*__Death and Dying: Attitudes of Patient and Doctor__ (S-11, 1965), Formulated by the Committee on Aging
*__Urban America and the Planning of Mental Health Services__ (S-10, 1964), Formulated by the Committee on Preventive Psychiatry
*__Pavlovian Conditioning and American Psychiatry__ (S-9, 1964), Formulated by the Committee on Research
*__Medical Uses of Hypnosis__ (S-8, 1962), Formulated by the Committee on Medical Education
*__Application of Psychiatric Insights to Cross-Cultural Communication__ (S-7, 1961), Formulated by the Committee on International Relations
*__The Psychological and Medical Aspects of the Use of Nuclear Energy__ (S-6, 1960), Formulated by the Committee on Social Issues
*__Some Considerations of Early Attempts in Cooperation Between Religion and Psychiatry__ (S-5, 1958), Formulated by the Committee on Psychiatry and Religion
*__Methods of Forceful Indoctrination: Observations and Interviews__ (S-4, 1957), Formulated by the Committee on Social Issues
*__Factors Used to Increase the Susceptibility of Individuals to Forceful Indoctrination: Observations and Experiments__ (S-3, 1956), Formulated by the Committee on Social Issues
*__Illustrative Strategies for Research in Psychopathology in Mental Health__ (S-2, 1956), Formulated by the Committee on Psychopathology
*__Considerations Regarding the Loyalty Oath as a Manifestation of Current Social Tension and Anxiety__ (S-1, 1954), Formulated by the Committee on Social Issues

Films

*__Discussion Guide to the Film__ (2, 1970)
*__A Nice Kid Like You__ (1, 1970)

Index

Absenteeism, 2, 12–13
Academy of Occupational and Organizational Psychiatry, 21
American Organization of Occupational Psychiatrists, 40
American Psychiatric Association Task Force on Occupational Psychiatry, 21
Anxiety, 2, 3, 14, 31
Authority issues, 19–20, 31
Availability, 2, 36–37

Biopsychosocial health advocacy, 35
Business school psychiatrist, 30–32

Career development, 23–34. *See also* Pathways into occupational psychiatry
Case examples
- of dyadic consultation, 3–4
- of expanded consultation, 7–9
- of liaison consultation, 4–7
- of strategic consultation, 12–14
- of team consultation, 10–11

Challenges, 17–23
- confidentiality concerns, 17–19
- due to psychiatrist's unresolved conflicts, 19–21
- due to scope of responsibilities, 21–22
- due to sense of inadequacy, 21–22
- resistance to dealing with psychiatrist, 17

Clinical flexibility, 38
Collaboration, 16
Communication, 2, 37
Confidentiality, 1, 9, 36
- employees' concerns about, 17–19

Conflict of interest, 18, 38
Consultation models, 1–14
- dyadic consultation, 3–4
- expanded consultation, 7–9
- liaison consultation, 4–7
- strategic consultation, 11–14
- team consultation, 9–11

Cooperation, 1
Coping skills, 14
Corporate irrationalities, 1–2
Corporate reorganization, 13–14
Cost effectiveness, xii–xiii
Countertransference issues, 20–21, 36

Depression, 2, 3, 14, 31
Disability evaluation, 24, 28
Duration of therapy, 3
Dyadic consultation, 3–4
- case example of, 3–4
- compared to traditional psychotherapy, 3, 4
- definition of, 2, 3
- duration of, 3

Dyadic consultation *(continued)*
referral for, 4
setting for, 3

Employee assistance program (EAP)
definition of, xiii
insurance payment for services of, 29
psychiatric leader of, 28–30
Employee-job fit, 6–7
Ethics, 34
Executive consultation, 32–33
Executive family course, 31
Executive job stress, 28
Expanded consultation, 7–9
case examples of, 7–9
definition of, 2, 7

Family issues, 46–47
Freud, Sigmund, 1
Future trends, 39–41

Goal setting, 37
Governmental organizations, 15
Grievances, 46
Group for the Advancement of Psychiatry, 63–86
Board of Directors, 73–75
Committee on Adolescence, 63
Committee on Aging, 63
Committee on Alcoholism and the Addictions, 63–64
Committee on Child Psychiatry, 64
Committee on College Students, 64
Committee on Cultural Psychiatry, 64
Committee on the Family, 64–65
Committee on Government Policy, 65
Committee on Handicaps, 65
Committee on Human Sexuality, 65
Committee on International Relations, 65–66
Committee on Medical Education, 66
Committee on Mental Health Services, 66
Committee on Occupational Psychiatry, 66
Committee on Planning and Communications, 67
Committee on Preventive Psychiatry, 67
Committee on Psychiatry and Religion, 68
Committee on Psychiatry and the Community, 67
Committee on Psychiatry and the Law, 67–68
Committee on Psychiatry in Industry, 21, 41
Committee on Psychopathology, 68
Committee on Public Education, 68
Committee on Research, 68
Committee on Social Issues, 69
Committee on Therapeutic Care, 69
Committee on Therapy, 69
contributing members, 70–72
Contributors, 75–76
Ginsburg Fellows, 69–70
life members, 72–73
Publications Board, 75
publications list, 77–86
Guidelines for occupational psychiatrist, 35–38
advocate biopsychosocial health, 35
avoid conflict of interest, 38

be available at all organizational levels, 36–37
be clinically flexible, 38
communicate clearly, 37
establish realistic goals, 37
explore transference and countertransference, 36
get supervision, 36
know your limitations, 38
know your role, 37–38
maintain confidentiality, 36
make use of team approach, 38
move slowly, 37
recognize individual versus organizational trade-offs, 37
review literature, 36
understand all components of organization, 36
understand "psychological contract," 35
Guilt
managerial, 17
"survivor," 14

Inadequacy, sense of, 21–22
Insurance reimbursement, 29
Interpersonal relationships, 15, 17
Introspection, 15

Job-finding strengths, 48
Job satisfaction, 45
Journal of Occupational Medicine, 34

Layoffs, 13–14
Leadership research, 25–26
Levels of intervention, 2
Liability litigation, 24
Liaison consultation, 4–7
case examples of, 4–7
definition of, 2, 4
referral for, 4
Limitations of occupational psychiatrist, 38
Literature on occupational psychiatry, 21, 36

"Managerial weakness," 17
Marital problems, 3–4, 31
Medical center psychiatrist, 27–28
Mentoring, 23–24
Mergers, 13–14
Morale problems, 2, 8–9, 13–14
Motivation, 11

Not-for-profit organizations, 15

Occupational psychiatrist
communicating availability of, 2
definition of, viii
guidelines for, 35–38
impact of unresolved conflicts of, 19–21
models of consultation for, 1–14
theoretical orientation of, 2
work and, x–xiii
Occupational psychiatry
challenges of, 17–23
compared to organizational psychiatry, vii
cost effectiveness of, xii–xiii
future trends affecting, 39–41
history of, viii–ix
pathways into, 23–34
rewards of, 15–17
Organizational culture, 15–16
Organizational development, 13–14
Organizational history, 49–56
analysis and conclusions, 55–56
description and analysis of current organization as a whole, 50–51
genetic data, 49–50

Organizational history *(continued)*
interpretive data, 51–55

Pathways into occupational psychiatry, 23–34
executive consultant, 32–33
founder of center for work and mental health, 33–34
private practitioner in business district, 26–27
psychiatric consultant to computer company, 24–25
psychiatric employee assistance program leader, 28–30
psychiatrist at business school, 30–32
psychiatrist at medical center, 27–28
researcher of leadership, 25–26
Power issues, 19–20, 31
Prejudice, 20
Preventive psychiatry, 32
Private practice, 26–27
Productivity, 2, 11
Profit-oriented organizations, 15–16
Psychiatric injuries in workplace, 34
"Psychological contract," 13, 35
Psychosomatic complaints, 14

Racism, 5
Referrals
confidentiality and, 18
for dyadic consultation, 3
for liaison consultation, 4
managerial motives for, 18
Resistance
corporate, 17
employee, 17–18
union, 19
Respect, 1
Rewards, 15–17
Role of occupational psychiatrist, 37–38

Scope of responsibilities, 21–22
Self-esteem, 4
Sexual harassment, 4–6
Social activities, 48
Stigma, 18
Strategic consultation, 11–14
boundaries for, 12
case examples of, 12–14
definition of, 2, 11
issues for, 11
Stress reduction, 10–11
Substance abuse, 30, 48
Supportive work environment, 9

Team approach, 38
Team consultation, 9–11
case example of, 10–11
definition of, 2, 10
Theoretical orientation, 2
Therapeutic alliance, 18, 20
Trade-offs, individual versus organizational, 37
Transference issues, 20–21, 36
Trust, 1, 9

Unemployment, 46
Unions, 19

Work
future trends affecting, 39–41
psychiatrist and, x–xiii
Work Force 2000: Work and Workers of the 21st Century, 39
Work history, psychiatric, 45–48
attitudes toward work, 46
financial issues, 46
grievances, 46
job satisfaction, 45

medical and psychiatric
disorders, 47
nature of job, 45
periods of disabilities or
substance abuse, 48
personal factors and work, 47
previous periods of
unemployment, 46
social activities, 48
work and family, 46–47
work and family of origin, 47
work and job-finding
strengths, 48
work career, 46
"Workaholism," 26–27
Worker's compensation, 24, 28

www.ingramcontent.com/pod-product-compliance
Ingram Content Group UK Ltd.
Pitfield, Milton Keynes, MK11 3LW, UK
UKHW020800290926
15470UKWH00008B/1836/J

9 780873 182065